8
Crucial
REALITIES

8
Crucial
REALITIES

Successful Choices for Graduates

Lissa Raines

PUBLISHING GROUP
Nashville, Tennessee

978-1-4336-7310-8

Published by B&H Publishing Group
Nashville, Tennessee

Dewey Decimal Classification: 248.83
Subject Heading: VOCATIONAL GUIDANCE \ SUCCESS \
CHRISTIAN LIFE

Unless otherwise noted all Scriptures are taken from the
New International Version (NIV), copyright © 1973, 1978, 1984 by
International Bible Society. Also used: New American Standard
Bible (NASB), Copyright © 1960, 1962, 1963, 1968, 1971, 1972, 1973,
1975, 1977, 1995 by The Lockman Foundation. Used by permission.

1 2 3 4 5 6 7 • 14 13 12 11

To my awesome husband, Doug, who has lavished on me an endless
supply of love and encouragement;
and
To my mother, Thelma "Terry" Dyer, who pointed me toward God's
reality when I was a child.

Thank you both for exemplifying His unconditional love.

For the Grad!

Date: _May 28, 2011_

To: _Leah Faulkner_

From: _Iowa Faulkners_

Message: _Happy future_
graduation!

Contents

Foreword: Governor Mike Huckabee   xi

Prologue: Life's Graduation Banquet   xiii

Introduction   1

SECTION I: RELATIONSHIP REALITIES

Quiz   7

Chapter 1: Password Your Heart   11

Chapter 2: Virus Alert *(Nine Items that Require Attention)*   17

Chapter 3: Spark to Flame   28

Overview   34

SECTION II: REALITIES OF GOD'S WILL

Quiz   39

Chapter 4: Traps to Avoid   43

Chapter 5: Uncloaking the Mystery   47

Chapter 6: Individual Leading   50

Overview   55

SECTION III: PERSONALITY REALITIES

Quiz   61

Chapter 7: Embrace Differences   65

Chapter 8: Personality Types   69

Chapter 9: Motivating Forces   77

Overview   81

SECTION IV: REAL AUTHORITY

Quiz   87

Chapter 10: Follow the Owner's Manual   90

Chapter 11: Choices and Consequences   95

Chapter 12: Secondhand Student 100
Overview 103

SECTION V: MONEY REALITIES

Quiz 109
Chapter 13: "Show Me the Money!" 113
Chapter 14: *Do's* and *Don'ts* 121
Chapter 15: Cons, Get-Rich-Quick Schemes, and Bad Ideas 127
Chapter 16: Money Habits of Successful People 133
Overview 138

SECTION VI: LIFESTYLE REALITIES

Quiz 143
Chapter 17: What You Feed Grows; What You Starve Dies 146
Chapter 18: Balanced Living for the Body, Mind, and Soul 151
Chapter 19: Slippery Slope 160
Overview 165

SECTION VII: THE DARK REALITY OF LIES

Quiz 171
Chapter 20: Types of Lies 174
Chapter 21: Lies Cost 182
Chapter 22: Truth Pays 185
Overview 188

SECTION VIII: SPIRITUAL REALITY

Quiz 193
Chapter 23: Trust the Alternate Reality 197
Chapter 24: God Is Near 204
Chapter 25: My Response 207
Overview 213

Epilogue: Life's Graduation Banquet, *continued* 217

Appendix I: Resources 221
Appendix II: Feed on God's Word 223
Appendix III: Things God Hates or Detests 229
Appendix IV: Quiz Answers 231

Foreword

By Governor Mike Huckabee

In *8 Crucial Realities* Lissa Raines encourages wise daily choices that create successful patterns and habits. Every choice, every decision has consequences. Your life direction is determined by one small decision here, one small decision there. If your choices are based on culture, your character is chipped away, one value at a time. The most destructive forces in the world are not "out there" somewhere, but inside your heart. By the same token, the most constructive forces in the world are not out there; they're internal. Your decisions determine your path, your success or failure in life.

Those who believe God created humans have a different worldview from those who believe humans created God. Our modern Christian culture has often adopted standards from those who place man at the center, rather than God at the center. One of the darkest times in the Old Testament was when man placed himself at the center: "Everyone did what was right in his own eyes" (Judg. 21:25 NASB). That is precisely where our culture is today. We have become a society of relativism and moral decay, losing our ability to navigate; we are drifting from the truth. In *8 Crucial Realities*, Raines provides a beacon of practical guidelines built on biblical principles to illuminate the graduate's path toward light and away from darkness— toward success and away from failure. The measure is not what culture says is right, but what God's principles require.

In *8 Crucial Realities* Raines encourages graduates to stretch themselves beyond the world's reality into God's reality where ultimate success is found. You, one individual, can touch the world. You can make a difference. The darker things are, the more difference even the tiniest light will make. Your spiritual light—your light of integrity, character, and a God-centered worldview—is just as invincible. We live in a dark spiritual age—it is my sincere hope that our culture's moral decline does not discourage you from fulfilling your potential. I hope that the great needs of this country will inspire you, our graduates, to become reformers, crusaders, leaders, governors—even presidents.

My career path has taken me from communications to pastorate to politics, giving me a broad perspective. Likewise, Lissa Raines' career path has been varied, taking this seminary graduate from ministry, to education, to counseling, to business. Her vast experience has illuminated common issues in our culture with which Christian graduates struggle. Whether the issue is money, relationships, or discovering God's will, you will find her practical advice and insights compelling and indispensible.

Prologue

Some of God's wisdom is self-evident and logical. Much of it is paradoxical and found only by seeking him. The journey toward God's light reality is a lifelong process. As we gain more wisdom and truth and, thus, more reality in our lives, we should strive to live up to what we already know. We should not lose sight of the basics as we delve deeper into God's mysteries and depth of understanding.

Unfortunately, even when we know truth and see clearly, we often decide we don't want to act in the way that we know is right. For various reasons, a choice that is out of line with God's reality may be more appealing. As we continue to choose against sound judgment, we lose sight of what is right and begin to believe a lie. Darkness is sure to follow.

Those in the light gain more soul wisdom and soul health, while those feasting in the dark experience "soul toll," sometimes without any knowledge of what is really taking place.

Life's Graduation Banquet

"The path of the righteous is like the first gleam of dawn, shining ever brighter till the full light of day. But the way of the wicked is like deep darkness; they do not know what makes them stumble." (Prov. 4:18–19)

He said, "Come." The voice echoed in my head. "Enter in," he implored.

So I entered the great banquet hall. The sign on the door read LIFE. Drapes of gold, silver, and burgundy adorned the walls. Grand chandeliers hung high above each table. Fountains bubbled over and around the ornately carved marble statues of exquisite, angelic creatures. Everywhere vibrant plants, trees, and flowers energized the room.

Many others had heard his call and had entered before me. They were already enjoying the delicacies before them—row after row of delicious meats and cheeses, fruits and vegetables, breads and desserts. Tables were adorned with costly linens and lace, and brightly colored flowers were scattered around each platter.

Most participants were totally engrossed in the delectable dishes. They hardly noticed the robed hosts gliding down each aisle, offering suggestions for nutritious and balanced eating. My eyes were drawn to the table full of chocolate. What a delightful surprise—my favorite. As I drew closer, I saw the nameplate on the table—"God's sweet presence." Yes, I understood. The food represented spiritual realities. As I wandered among the tables, I saw "Fellowship," "Brokenness," "Compassion," "Prayer," "Peace," "Reconciliation," and "Honesty." What a wonderful smorgasbord, and I had only just begun to investigate.

A sign over the aisle leading to the back read "Free Will." A most enjoyable gift—the liberty to choose. My curiosity rose, and I decided to delay eating and take a closer look around. I hesitated, not wanting to leave the area that housed these wonderful delicacies, but decided to follow the aisle that read "Free Will." The farther I proceeded, the darker and gloomier the hall became. I wondered if the power was out in the back area. The plants and trees were withered, and the fountains were dry. The only light in that section emanated from the robed hosts who offered, but didn't force, guidance on healthy eating. Across their robes, different names were embroidered in silver and gold. Close enough to read were James, John, Proverbs, and Revelation. There were dozens of hosts around the banquet hall, all quietly speaking their wisdom. As they opened their mouths, a fluid light poured forth on and around the person with whom they were speaking. It was almost as if the words had a life of their own. So that was it; the hosts were speaking God's words of wisdom.

Suddenly, a light breeze interrupted my musing. What was the stench that assaulted me? It was incredible—like a combination of vomit, rotten eggs, and pig farm. As I proceeded, I couldn't believe my eyes. Many were feasting on decaying food, sour milk, maggots, worms, manure, and even vomit—gorging themselves until they became sick and then returning for more filth.

I couldn't understand it. The banquet hall was filled with fabulous delicacies, yet many were choosing these gross alternatives. Even more amazing was their deception. They thought they were eating fresh, juicy fruit and rich desserts. I heard one declare, "This mango is incredibly succulent." Another proclaimed, "This Key lime pie is to die for!"

As I perused the tables, I saw more nameplates, just as I had when I first entered. On the first table, the nameplate read, "Lust." It was next to "Adultery." Then there were "Greed" and "Selfishness." On the next table were "Lies" and "Deception." The table "Pride" was followed by "Arrogance." "Gossip" and "Slander" were close by.

"How can this be?" I asked one of the robed hosts.

He replied, "Look carefully at those who have chosen these tables."

My focus turned from the overpowering, putrid food to the people enjoying it. It was then I noticed that many had a layered, white film over their eyes. They were blind; they could not see what they were eating. But surely they could taste and smell it. One of the robed hosts seemed to know what I was thinking. He explained, "From years of eating the wrong foods, they have acquired a taste for the putrid. What once repulsed them no longer does."

Their bodies were emaciated, like those you see starving in drought-stricken lands. They could choose the absolute best, but they desired the worst. And they were literally starving to death because of it. How incredible. Why would God allow this path of free will if it led to this?

A strong, fresh wind blew through the area. I allowed myself to be guided gently toward an aisle leading back to the light. The sign over this aisle also read "Free Will." In small letters below those words, "Fear of the Lord" glowed. So free will led to the best, and free will led to the worst. The same gift—drastically different results.

Some were running in circles—coming in and gorging on the rancid food, and then running out and feasting on the wholesome food. But they didn't look well either. They were not as thin and frail as the totally blind who willingly stayed in the dark. But every time the vacillating participants ate from the tables in the dark, another set of chains descended from the shadows, binding and constraining them just a little more. And each time they indulged in the detestable, another thin layer shrouded their eyes. Because their sight was impaired, they constantly bumped into those around them and lost their balance. With their awkward movements, they were doing considerable damage to those in the light, tripping and knocking them down.

To be continued—see epilogue.

Introduction

Congratulations! You have graduated. Now what? You are on your own, with the rest of your life ahead of you. What will it hold? Will you be successful? More importantly, how will you measure success? Do you think success is being rich, powerful, and famous? Or is success living a life of purpose, with great relationships and as little self-imposed heartache as possible? If you believe it is the latter, then this book is for you. If you believe it is the former, then you'll need to buy a different book.

Whether you are a high school, university, or graduate school graduate, you will be facing new challenges and opportunities in the coming days. Each graduation brings with it new levels of independence and life-changing realities. *Eight Crucial Realities* will explore areas that will sustain successful living at home, work, and school (should you pursue further education). Schools today focus more on practical living than they used to, but many basic principles of success are still missing from the curriculum, especially in the realities of the soul and day-to-day living.

We all have our perception of reality, and to some extent that perception creates our life as we know it because our behavior is typically based on our beliefs. But believing something doesn't necessarily make it so. Embracing false perceptions hinders us from acting and living in sync with the truth—if we misbelieve, we misbehave. This makes life harder. We live crosswise to principles of ultimate reality that make our path easier to navigate. Acting on false perceptions clouds true reality, and the consequences can be grim. We don't end up where we want to go.

When the wrong address has been entered in our GPS, we end up at the wrong destination. We think we entered it correctly; we think we are headed in the right direction, but we arrive somewhere else. While visiting in Missouri recently, we stayed at a condo in Branson West. Relatives had arranged to meet us there. They entered Branson instead of Branson West in their GPS and, consequently, went on a wild goose chase looking for our condo. Time was wasted, and frustration was high because their GPS was not programmed with the correct address. Believing it was the right address didn't make it so. Try as they might, they were not able to arrive at the right destination with the wrong address programmed in. The GPS' reality was wrong. Likewise, if you follow a false reality, you will not arrive at the successful destination you desire.

Having counseled and advised thousands of individuals, I have observed the same mistakes being made over and over, most often in ignorance of the wisdom that could have saved them from much heartache and stagnation. Mistakes and false realities exist in everyone's life. Part of the process of successful living is to reveal and then discard the false ideas we have held. Only then can we discover and live in the truth. We must "renew" our minds.

Proverbs 23:7 clearly states, "For as he thinks within himself, so he is" (NASB). Many of our thoughts and attitudes seem to be small in the scheme of life, but it is the small things in life that produce our substance and character. As we shape our beliefs and values, we shape our future and the impact we will have on those around us. Each section of this book starts with some true/false questions and multiple choice stories—so you can gage what you believe now. As you read the chapter, you may rethink some of the issues and deep-seated paradigms that have been instilled by our culture. Even a slight shift in our thinking can bring great results in our lives. After each section there are additional questions about that reality. This book will benefit you most if you take a little time to answer each question and then take the steps to produce success. A lot of little changes over time will yield great dividends in your future.

Practical and spiritual topics are included, but the practical are largely encompassed in the spiritual. Whether we are aware of it or not, spiritual principles often determine our day-to-day choices and attitudes. The practical chapters deal with personalities, relationships, money, and lifestyles. Wisdom in these areas is often culturally affected, so specifics of contemporary life are taken into account and often influence the wisest, most successful decisions. The spiritual topics focus on wisdom of the soul and spirit that transcend our culture, but affect it nonetheless. They include authority, lies, God's will and spiritual realities.

While we often think life is happening to us, we each have the great gift of choice that can make all the difference. This reality was vividly illustrated as I watched the seagulls on the ocean waves this morning. Typically, they bask in the sun on the water beyond the crashing waves, but this morning they were floating among the breaking waves, lifting off right before the next wave crashed down on them. Then they would land again, just in time to lift off to avoid another oncoming wave. Most of the time they avoided the crash, but every so often, the waves came sooner than anticipated, toppling them in every direction into the dark water below. It was quite a sight as they frantically lifted, landed, lifted, landed and then occasionally crashed. I wondered why they didn't just rest beyond the breaking waves, for tranquility was only a few yards away.

Like the seagulls, we often choose to settle in the darkness of turmoil and trouble rather than in the light of peace and tranquility. The safe zone is close by; often, it is even in view. Most of the time, the gulls rescued themselves and rose above the next crash, but if they stayed too long, the waves would eventually catch them and hurl them wing over wing into the dark water. All they had to do to avoid this trouble was move. They didn't even have to move very far, but they did have to move. They had to choose to relocate.

It is easy to understand physical analogies. If the crashing wave is threatening our safety, we get out or stay out of the way. But in the realm of the soul, we can't see, touch, smell or taste the reality of being in the wrong place, so we are much more likely to stay there, wander there, or be sucked into a dangerous dark area where we are bombarded with wave after wave of turmoil.

Many unseen realities surround our souls. We can deliberately seek, find, and walk in them, or we can continue on a dark path, finding ourselves lost. The sooner we realize success in life is found in God's truth, the sooner we stop paying the cost of walking in false realities. It is not difficult, but it does take effort and decisive action, for walking in truth is not natural; it is only accomplished on purpose. Not making a deliberate choice to walk in reality is a passive choice to walk in the darkness—a choice that will cost us "soul toll," the price we pay for unwise decisions.

If you have made some bad decisions, you may not be able to undo the repercussions or consequences, but you can move forward living your life in such a way that the surf is not endlessly crashing down on you, plunging you into darkness where there is confusion and pain. You can gain the awareness that will help you to navigate the challenges of life and successfully travel in reality.

Graduates, you are now on your way to a new life—a life of independence and fulfillment. The outcome depends largely on you. You make choices. You develop habits and attitudes. You live with the consequences. Your life choices will determine who you are, who you become, and whether or not your life is successful. Choose wisely.

SECTION I: RELATIONSHIP REALITIES

Quiz

Multiple Choice Stories

Choose the *best* answer to the questions below.

1. After waiting for six months, Samantha has her wish. She is dating charming, intelligent and handsome Anthony. They both love travelling, politics, and community involvement. He is one year ahead of her in law school and has the remarkable ambition of being the president of the United States one day. He has teased her about being his "first lady." While flattered, she has begun to have nagging feelings about the relationship. Anthony can be rude and disrespectful toward those with disabilities or disadvantages. He acts superior in their presence and mocks them behind their back. He also treats his family poorly, though he is great to Samantha, making her feel like a queen.

She should _____.

    a. break up with him. Rudeness to the disadvantaged and poor treatment of family are red flags of character issues and give Samantha good reason to end the relationship.

    b. not worry about it because he is treating her right. Anthony is the first boyfriend who opens doors for her, buys her expensive gifts, and obviously places her on a pedestal.

    c. counsel him about his bad behavior. Since he is so good to her, she knows he can be kind; he just needs a little encouragement. She should hang on to him; he has rare potential and ambition.

d. hang in there a little longer and see if her kind treatment of others rubs off on him. After all, we become like those with whom we associate.

2. Elizabeth is in a dry spell in her relationship with Ryan. They have been married for three years and are growing apart. They don't find their relationship fun or fulfilling like they did when they were first married. The camping trips, hiking and kayaking they enjoyed together are in the past. Life has become routine, predictable, and boring. Both are busy with their careers and though they don't have children yet, they don't spend much time together.

They should _____.

a. divorce now before kids are in the picture.

b. find ways to rekindle the spark—more quality time together, weekends away, talking, touching, and focusing on the positive in each other.

c. seek out a counselor to help bring a resolution to their dissatisfaction.

d. b or c, depending on the seriousness of the problem.

3. Cody and Jasmine dated for two years and sacrificially supported each other through their challenging medical internships. A short time later, Jasmine lost both of her parents in a car accident. Through these trials Cody and Jasmine's love grew stronger, so they decided to marry. However, after just one month of marriage, Cody wonders what happened to sweet, supportive Jasmine. She is frequently angry and has even been abusive at times, throwing pots, pans, cell phones, and even a hot curling iron at him. He is embarrassed about his bruises and marks, so he lies to his friends.

Cody should _____.

a. seek counseling immediately. The longer this behavior continues, the worse it will get. They need outside help.

b. do nothing. He is a man, so he should take it. After all, he is bigger and stronger than she is. He should realize she is just reacting to the death of her parents.

c. fight back. She started it. If she gets a taste of her own medicine, she will stop.

d. enlist the support of friends and family for an intervention to confront Jasmine about her bad behavior. The shock value and humiliation will motivate her to change her ways.

TRUE OR FALSE?

Relationship Realities

True/False 1. How a person I'm dating treats a waitress doesn't reflect how that person will treat me.

True/False 2. If you find the right person, you will find happiness and your relationship will be healthy.

True/False 3. It is reasonable to expect your spouse to change to make you happy.

True/False 4. It is best to marry a person who is very different from you, so that person can "complete" you.

True/False 5. It is wise to date non-Christians because they may come to believe through you.

True/False 6. Even if family and friends are against you marrying someone, you should proceed if you really love the person.

True/False 7. True love will overcome any obstacles you face in your relationship.

True/False 8. If an addict or abuser sincerely promises to change, it is appropriate to move forward in your relationship.

True/False 9. If you discover the person you are dating lies, it isn't that big a deal because everyone lies.

True/False 10. Feelings of romantic love should not be the primary foundation for a marriage.

1

Password Your Heart

"Above all else, guard your heart,
for it is the wellspring of life." (Prov. 4:23)

When we have an important file on our computer, we password protect it. If we didn't, it could be open to theft and invasion. It is critical to protect it because we consider it valuable. But do we value our heart as much? Scripture places great worth on our heart, saying it is the wellspring of life. The *Merriam-Webster's* dictionary defines wellspring as "a source of continual supply." So the heart is a continual supply of life. That sounds rather important. Of course, in this context the heart is not the physical heart, but the emotional heart. Good emotional "heart" health is crucial to our overall well-being. Why not ensure some protection by passwording your heart with guidelines before your heart is pirated by a thief?

It is true; love is blind, deaf, and dumb. When we are emotionally involved—worse still if we are also physically involved—with "the one," we lose much objectivity, and our brains seem to become mush. The common sense that seemed so obvious when our friend was in a relationship is now absent. We rationalize away character and personality issues that could cause havoc in a committed permanent relationship. Romantic love is a key theme in countless books, movies, and songs, and it brings about some of our most stupid mistakes in life—causing untold soul toll.

General Guidelines

Time Factor

Know (preferably date or court) the person for at least a year. While this guideline is just that, it is helpful to observe a person over a long period of time to discover who they truly are. Everyone, consciously or otherwise, tries to make a good impression. Most often trying to make an impression is not a deliberate deception; the person is just trying to charm you into that second, third, and fourth date.

If someone is deliberately putting up a façade, it will be impossible to maintain it indefinitely. The true self will become evident—if given enough time. The more you see your "true love" interacting with other people, the more you will be able determine his or her true character.

Does he respect those in authority—his boss and the government—including law enforcement? While most of us have some opinion on how those over us can improve and do a better job, a person of character will submit to those in authority without always looking for a loophole or exception. This doesn't refer to those who are being proactive to improve society, but to those who think they are "above" the law. Rebellion and pride are sure relationship destroyers. Don't overlook this "macho" stance that some people take with authority. It may be enticing now, but it reveals some underlying character issues that will eventually surface.

How does she treat strangers? Is she kind and respectful, or rude and unconcerned with others' feelings? How does he treat the waitress, the clerk at the store, or the person who stops him on the street? Is she cruel to animals? Does he make fun of people with disabilities or who are less fortunate? These behaviors will reveal deeper character issues.

Though some have the gift of "helping others" (1 Cor. 12:28) and are particularly focused on meeting people's needs, we all should be kind to those around us (Gal. 5:22). God imparts differing spiritual gifts, but he grows the same fruit of the spirit in all of his children, regardless of gifting or natural personality preferences. Look for good fruit—love, joy, peace, patience, kindness, goodness, faithfulness, gentleness and self-control.

Password: Time

Family Focus

People are most genuine around those they know best and with whom they feel most comfortable—their family. Typically, a person doesn't feel the need to impress or "earn" respect within his family. He is usually loved, flaws and all. So it is important to see how a person interacts with parents, siblings, and children (if he or she is a parent). Does he treat you differently than he treats his family of origin or his children? If he treats you better than he treats his family, his attitude may change when he makes a deeper commitment to you. Usually, when you step into the role of family, you will be treated like family.

If the person is constantly critical of those closest to her, beware. Negativity and constant criticism can crush the spirit of those on whom it is inflicted. If a person always seems to be "using" family members' time, energy, and help without reciprocating, she could be a taker rather than a giver. If she is on bad terms with everyone in her immediate family, beware. Habits she exhibits in her family of origin often will be transferred into her own marriage, even if those things are not evident while dating. You must decide what you can and cannot tolerate.

While a dysfunctional family of origin does not necessarily determine one's fate, it does bring a whole system of learned behavior that is hard to break. No one is able to choose his or her family of origin, and many people rise above the dysfunction of their family, sometimes with the help of a counselor. If your prospective mate is from a clearly dysfunctional family, make sure his or her interactions have risen above the family standard. If not, chances are he or she will carry that dysfunction into your newly created family should the two of you marry.

Password: Family

Not a Panacea

The world is looking for love. At the top of love's list is romantic love. It's promoted in movies, ads, and books. I am a big fan of mystery novels, and without fail there is a budding romance as a secondary plot in every mystery. Somehow, romantic love is supposed to be a cure-all and bring happiness into our lives. We all want to feel good and find contentment. Unfortunately, the world has convinced us that if we just find Mr. or Miss Right, happiness will follow. Because romantic love creates such strong feelings, it is assumed to be the ultimate path to happiness.

The giddy infatuation ("being in love" feelings) will wax and wane, and if there was no happiness before the relationship, there will be no happiness after those feelings fade. Not to say we can't have ongoing romantic feelings for our love interest, but the feelings described on the *Mr. Deeds* "Hallmark" card are temporary: "Hard to breathe, feels like floating, So full of love my heart's exploding, Mouth is dry, hands are shaking, My heart is yours for the taking, Acting weird, not myself, Dancing around like the Keebler elf, Finally time for this poor schlub, To know how it feels to fall in lub" It is not a very eloquent or romantic portrayal of romance, but it is descriptive. Thankfully, it is not a permanent state.

We must know happiness as a single person to know true happiness when we marry. If we look to another person to make us happy, we set ourselves up for disappointment and are placing unrealistic expectations on another human being. Think about it: Do you want to be the sole source of another human's happiness? That is a lot of pressure. And even if you wanted to, you could never fill all of another's needs. Since we don't want to, and couldn't fulfill another person's happiness, we should not place that expectation or burden on others. We must follow God's directions for true happiness—living our life as God intended in relationship with him and other believers.

Password: Reality

Don't Expect Him (or Her) to Change

Many people enter marriage expecting their partner to change. The sports fanatic or wild shopper they are planning to marry is still the sports fanatic or wild shopper after they are married. It is unfair to pledge yourself to someone, knowing he is a certain way and then expect him to change for you after you marry. You certainly wouldn't appreciate that yourself.

While we all grow and change, hopefully for the better, it is not something that can be accomplished from the outside. You cannot make another person change. Sure, you may gain compliance in behavior, but that is not a true change of the heart. That must come from within. The Holy Spirit is the one who convicts of sin, and the Father gives the grace to repent and change the core of our being.

Sometimes we desire to see a change that is not a moral or spiritual change. We shouldn't be praying or hoping our partner will be someone other than who God made her to be. To desire that an introvert become an extrovert or a person who loves numbers and science to deeply appreciate art and literature is unfair and unlikely to ever occur. We should not attempt to make over our partner in our image. When differences cause friction, both can compromise and move toward a comfortable workable solution without changing the core of the other person's being.

Password: Contentment

Opposites Attract and Drive Each Other Crazy!

It is true that opposites often attract. When someone is different from us, often we find that difference intriguing. The person seems to balance us, complete us, and make us whole. Years later, those very things that attracted us may drive us apart and drive us crazy!

Andrea, who is carefree and for whom life is always a fun adventure was very attractive to serious, meticulous Jason, who is ultra-responsible. While they were dating he was drawn to her humor and easygoing attitude. He was fascinated by the joy and adrenaline rush she got from parachuting, rock climbing, and whitewater rafting. Andrea was attracted to Jason's grounded life in the real world, where bills have to be paid and food put on the table. She appreciated him as her rock, someone who was always steady and stable, who didn't need anyone. They appeared to be the perfect match.

Several years have passed since they married, and now Jason wishes Andrea would be more serious and responsible instead of living for the next safari or cruise. She wishes he'd lighten up and join her in life's adventure; she feels life is too short not to enjoy it. Of course, he may be enjoying life, just not by her definition. Did either of them change after they married? No. Their perspective of the each other changed as they settled into day-to-day living.

The "being in love" feeling is transient, and when it wanes, the rose-colored glasses become clear. The things that originally drew a couple together may then push them apart. Ironic, isn't it? Jason loved Andrea's carefree attitude. Now he sees her as irresponsible, with her head in the clouds. She loved his macho, self-made man attitude, and now she feels he is too detached, unemotional, and not much fun.

Be aware of what draws you to your love. Is it something that ultimately will push you away from him? Try to look at yourself from his perspective. Are you a super extrovert who loves to have people around all the time? Is he a super introvert who loves the fact that you carry him in social situations? Will he be able to tolerate having a lot of friends around and attending frequent social gatherings? Will you be able to tolerate the amount of alone time your partner needs? These types of questions are not often asked before marriage because initially these differences appear to be attractive, not problems. They tend to cause trouble over the long term rather than the short term.

People can and will change, but you cannot go into marriage assuming or expecting the person to be different ten years from now. You are marrying who he is today, and that needs to be enough. If you need him to change for you to be happy, do not marry him. It is not fair to you or to him.

The good news is that, if you are married, you can change your attitude and that will make you much happier! Remember who your spouse was when you first married. Remember why those same qualities that bug you now attracted you then. Focus on all of her positive qualities, not on the things you don't like. If you refocus your perspective to the positive, you will more readily be able to have a grateful heart. If glaring character deficiencies exist, not just differences, remember that there is hope. God answers prayer. Conviction by the Holy Spirit, as well as a life well lived in front of someone with real flaws can be motivation for the person to change.

Password: Acceptance

Spiritual Compatibility

You take a great risk if you date someone who is not a believer. The longer you stay in the relationship, the harder it is to leave and the more you grow attached to the person. Second Corinthians 6:14 clearly tells us, "Do not be yoked together with unbelievers." Life is difficult enough. Don't add the complication of marrying someone without the same foundation of faith and the Bible. It is possible that an unbelieving spouse may become a believer, but you can't count on that happening. Remember, you must be happy with the way your spouse is when you marry. If you are not, don't marry the person. While you don't have to believe every doctrine exactly the same, you both must agree on the basic tenants. If you are from different denominations or churches, it is healthy to agree on a church or denomination you will both attend when you marry and to which you will eventually bring your children when they are born.

While many people in the world in healthy relationships do not adhere to Christianity, it is important for you, if you are a Christian, to find a Christian mate. The Christian world outlook is unique. If you desire to base your life on what is written in God's word, someone who doesn't believe may draw you away from God's ways rather than encourage you in your faith and Christian growth. If you have children together, do you want them to live in a house divided against itself on spiritual issues? If you are a believer, you will not want to raise your children that way.

Before you say, "I do," it is wise to enter pre-marriage counseling with a Christian counselor or clergy member. They have been trained to raise issues that you and your honey may not have considered. It is best to go into marriage with your eyes wide open and with no major surprises in expectations or lifestyles. If no red flags surface, counseling should give you the confidence to move forward, building your relationship on a great common foundation—your relationship with God and belief in his word.

Password: Spiritual

2

Virus Alert *(Nine Items that Require Attention)*

"The prudent man sees danger and takes refuge, but the simple keep going and suffer for it." (Prov. 22:3)

If you have installed Norton, McAfee, or other software for virus and spyware protection, your computer will warn you when there is a potentially detrimental or invasive force in it. Unfortunately, we do not have an innate virus alert to detect when destructive elements have entered our relationship. Consider the following risks seriously before you commit to marry someone. If you believe the relationship is mostly good, try counseling before you exit. But if there are damaging issues that you know will remain, save yourself from the darkness and gracefully let go of the relationship. Life is short. You don't want to spend it weighed down by a person who is unwilling or unable to change. Over time, major relationship challenges will wear on your health, emotions, and spirit. Do you really want to pay the soul toll?

Nagging Feelings

Beware if you have unresolved nagging feelings about the relationship. Regarding business, Dr. Henry Cloud calls this the *cringe factor*.[1] If you have to cringe when you think about a certain aspect of the person, listen to your doubt; do not go forward. Visit a pre-marriage counselor and

---

1. Dr. Henry Cloud, *9 Things You Simply Must Do to Succeed in Love and Life* (Integrity Publishers: Brentwood, TN, 2004), 65.

work out any concerns before you get married. It is easier to separate now if issues are not resolved than to go through a divorce or live unhappily.

It is not that you should see no fault in the other person. If you are in a healthy relationship, you will know their weaknesses and faults as well as their strengths. We all have both. But if there are things that really bother you, and you know they will cause ongoing trouble, wait to commit until these are settled. Do not accept their word that they will change. Good intentions are just that. The proof is in the enduring fruit of their life over time.

Alert: Stop

Warnings from Friends and Family

Beware if family and friends think you should not marry the person. Slow way down until there is a general consensus that you are making a good decision. God has given us each other as objective observers when it comes to love. Not everyone in your life has to love the person as much as you do, but most of the significant people in your life should support the marriage. They will more easily be able to discern motive and character than you will, since your judgment is likely clouded by emotions. Most often, friends and family have known you longer than your potential mate has, and they can offer you objective opinions about your relationship.

Alert: Question

Control Issues

Beware if your love interest puts limits on time spent with family and friends. Put on the breaks. This is a classic sign of an abuser. A healthy person will not be possessive of all your time and energy, nor try to keep you away from those who love and support you. We all need many people in our lives in order to be whole and happy. Also beware if your potential spouse is overly controlling about what you wear, what you do in your free time, or how you spend your money. These issues of control will only get worse after you are married, for then your spouse may feel he has a right to tell you what to do. If he always has to make the decisions regarding your lives and is offended when you want something different, beware. A mild case of "control" may be personality related and easily worked out with willing hearts and, if necessary, a good counselor, but more serious control issues that denote abusive relationships should make you question whether to stay in the relationship. Such patterns are not easily changed.

Alert: Reconsider

Addictions

"For where your treasure is,
there your heart will be also." (Matt. 6:21)

Beware if your significant other engages in substance abuse or has a gambling or sexual addiction, but promises to change. True addictions do not just go away. A person must first admit that she is an addict and seek outside help. There are support groups for alcoholics, drug abusers, sex addicts, and compulsive gamblers. Encourage her to get involved in one of these. In order to get past her addiction, she must associate with those who will help her, rather than those who drag her down. See Appendix I for resources.

If you decide to stay in the relationship, attend Al-Anon meetings or another support group for those involved with addicts. By doing this you will know how to best help her and not become part of the problem. An addict typically does not want to hurt the people in her life. When she promises to change, she is sincere, but without power when she tries to stop on her own. Only with God and others can she conquer the addiction and move on to a healthy life. Do not marry her until she has proven over time that she has made a lasting change. To do otherwise is to bring great darkness into your life.

Alert: Hazard

Drastic Mood Swings

"A man of understanding is even-tempered." (Prov. 17:27)

Beware if your love has severe mood changes. Do not marry him until he gets help and there is a long-term difference. A number of reasons could be at the root; unresolved, there is not a good foundation for a solid relationship. If you think the inconsistency in his emotional state is due to a physical disorder, encourage him to visit his doctor for an official diagnosis; the doctor may recommend a good psychiatrist. A chemical imbalance can often be treated with medication.

It is difficult, if not impossible, to maintain a stable relationship if one person has extreme moods. Life can be unsettling with a sweetheart who is Dr. Jekyll some days and Mr. Hyde other days. In Robert Louis Stevenson's story *Strange Case of Dr. Jekyll and Mr. Hyde*, Dr. Jekyll was a pleasant, upstanding citizen, while Mr. Hyde was a violent, conscience-free murderer.

Hopefully, your love is not as radical as that, but he may be so different at times that you feel he could be a different individual. If affected with bipolar disorder, he may swing from excited and enthusiastic to depressed and irritable. Or if his mood changes in an instant from calmness to rage, take a step back and consider whether you want to live your life walking on eggshells, never sure what is coming next. Living with such a person will keep you off-balance emotionally and will destroy your trust, not to mention your feelings of security and self-esteem.

Alert: Run

Violence/Abuse

"An angry man stirs up dissension, and a hot-tempered one commits many sins." (Prov. 29:22)

Beware if your love exhibits signs of violence or abuse. If he is physically hostile in one area of his life, there is a good chance he will bring it home. Do not tolerate violent behavior from anyone. Seek to remove yourself as quickly as possible from the situation, and if you are injured, press charges. While abusers try to convince their victims that the abuse is their fault, do not buy into that. There is no excuse for someone to be violent with you or your children.

A person who uses violence against others has some very deep issues that need to be resolved. Typically, he is not going to get better without outside intervention. As with addictions, he must first recognize and admit he has a problem. Until that happens, there will be no change. If you are not in a serious relationship, it is best to move on. Direct him toward help and proceed with your life. If you are married to an abuser, there is hope. Because of the commitment you made, you should stay with him—as long as possible if he is seeking help, though not necessarily under the same roof. If it is dangerous for you or your children to be with him, find other accommodations. If you have no place to go, confide in your church leadership and see if they can arrange something, or check into local shelters for battered women and children. On occasion, the woman is the batterer. The same advice holds true for men: Remove yourself from the situation.

Do not just hope things will get better on their own. They will not. Typically, they get worse, and staying in a relationship without bringing any outside influences will only result in you enabling his abuse. You become part of the problem. If he is abusing the children, by all means take them out of the situation and protect them. They can't do this for themselves.

Kayla and Matt were married for three years when Marissa came along. A year later, Heather was born. While Matt had exhibited some immature behavior and a short fuse before the children were born, he hadn't abused Kayla physically. So Kayla was shocked when he began to have episodes of rage in which he hurt the girls. Most adults expect children to behave in immature irresponsible ways. But when Marissa and Heather were fussy or acting like children, Matt hit them repeatedly, leaving bruises and welts. Occasionally he drew blood or caused swelling. His frustration and anger were unjustified and out of control.

Kayla had committed her life to Christ when she was young and didn't believe in divorce. She reasoned that if she prayed hard enough, God would protect her children. But as they grew older the abuse continued. A neighbor reported Matt to DFS for child abuse, but instead of seeing it as a wake-up call, he ranted and raved about being persecuted because he was a Christian. He felt he was no different than any other man. He rationalized that his irrational anger was normal.

Unfortunately, when Marissa was eight she began to talk about suicide. She was very afraid of her dad and felt she was never good enough for him. Marissa was a typical girl, active and eager to please. She was a straight-A student and in no sense a troublemaker or unruly child. She just really wanted her dad to be proud of her. Marissa began to have nightmares and become hysterical when she was startled. She was exhibiting signs of child abuse. Heather began to regress and at five years old wanted Kayla to feed and dress her. She also became hysterical when startled.

Though Kayla had prayed earnestly, God hadn't protected the girls from reality. He was counting on Kayla to do that. She was an adult in authority over her children. When a friend confronted her with her responsibility and the fact she was enabling an abuser, she crumbled. She couldn't believe she hadn't realized that it was her responsibility to protect her children from her spouse. She was part of the problem.

This is often the case in Christian homes. A person will stay in an unhealthy, dangerous relationship because she believes it is the Christian thing to do. God does not expect us to live with abuse toward ourselves or our children. This includes emotional, verbal, and physical abuse. They may occur in isolation, but often go hand in hand. The first step is to seek outside help. If help is not wanted or sought, it is right to separate (or if dating, to break up). It is better than staying and enabling a person to continue to sin and bring untold damage and darkness on yourself and your family.

Some stay in abusive relationships because they are beaten down emotionally and feel they are getting what they deserve, or they may believe that if they leave the abuser, they will be alone for the rest of their life. The thought of being alone is often worse than being with someone who abuses them. Abuse has become normal, and until the pain of the abuse is greater than the pain of being alone, they will stay. If this is you, do not allow yourself to hit rock bottom in the relationship before you separate. Stop stealing future joy from yourself!

Alert: Danger

Extreme Selfishness/Pride

"Do nothing out of selfish ambition or vain conceit, but in humility consider others better than yourselves." (Phil. 2:3)

Beware if your love is consumed with herself. If most conversations are about what *she* has done, what *she* is doing and planning, or how *she* feels, move on. Selfish people often exhibit a confident and charismatic personality, which may initially seem enchanting, charming, or exciting. Given enough time, their selfishness will become obvious. While we are all by nature somewhat selfish, two people need to be important to two people for the relationship to work.

If the love of your life has little time for your friends or interests, beware. Of course, you both need to have some time apart, but if your love can never make it to any of your family gatherings or holidays or the children's events (if you have children), then he may be too wrapped up in himself for a successful or serious relationship. This is especially true if he finds lots of time for his friends and family and interests, but not for yours. The selfish person is different from the controlling person in that he doesn't mind if you spend time with your friends, family and interests, as long as you don't expect him to join you.

The selfish person often latches on to someone who is giving and self-sacrificing; a relationship between two selfish people would blow up very quickly. Neither would be willing to give up their selfish priorities, and they would go their separate ways. If you are a nurturing, giving person by nature, beware of those who would take advantage of your selfless personality.

Selfishness is sometimes combined with a large dose of unhealthy pride. The person feels entitled to be treated better than everyone else. Rules are for other people; she deserves the exception or break. Be careful if she always needs to be right. Such a person cannot stand it when you disagree. She wants total compliance and may become angry if you don't accept what she says as gospel. Beware; you cannot have a relationship when the person refuses to allow you to express your ideas and opinions. In healthy relationships, we learn from each other as "iron sharpens iron" (Prov. 27:17). Discussion and dialogue between two people with open hearts and minds can greatly benefit both. No one perfectly understands everything. When one person has the only opinion that counts, you no longer have a relationship, but a dictatorship. "Pride only breeds quarrels, but wisdom is found in those who take advice" (Prov. 13:10).

Alert: Threat

Neediness

It may be flattering for someone to call you ten times a day, send you three hundred text messages, e-mail you thirty-five times, and want to spend every waking hour he possibly can with you, but it is not healthy. That attention will soon turn to feeling smothered and responsible for his happiness. That is not a fair place for anyone. A clingy, needy person is not someone who will enhance your life; he will eventually drain your energy and cause resentment.

While it is natural, particularly in the early stages of a relationship, to spend a massive amount of time contacting each other, it is not a good place to stay. You need to maintain your friendships, hobbies, family relationships, time at church, and daily routines to have a healthy life. The adage that absence makes the heart grow fonder is true. Having a well-rounded, balanced life will make your times together more meaningful. You both need some alone time, as well, in order to grow as individuals.

Some say a significant other "completes" you, but that would indicate anyone without a partner is incomplete, which is just not true. If that were the case, Jesus would not have been a complete individual, and we know he was the most complete individual to walk the earth. While we all need people in our lives, we must be whole before we are in a serious relationship. God and his family complete us. He gives us his spirit, his word, and his children to bring us life and spiritual understanding.

A loving relationship is one of the most wonderful things in the world to experience, but it is not a requirement to be whole or happy. A better concept is that the right significant other can enlarge your life, not complete it. Just as having children opens up new areas of experience and life, a partner can do likewise. But many are complete and whole without a spouse or a child. You must see yourself as whole prior to a relationship for a healthy, serious relationship to flourish.

Alert: Detach

Compulsive Lying

**"Truthful lips endure forever, but a lying tongue lasts
only a moment. The Lord detests lying lips, but he delights
in men who are truthful." (Prov. 12:19, 22)**

Beware if you don't know when your love is lying or telling the truth. In today's society lying has become standard practice. Rather than taking responsibility for their choices and actions, people lie. In order to avoid hurting someone's feelings, people lie (we've all been tempted and probably succumbed in this area). To avoid negative consequences or someone's disapproval, people lie. And then there are those who just lie about everything and anything for no apparent reason. See chapter 20, for a more in-depth discussion about types of lies. While all lying is unhealthy and destructive, the compulsive liar lies out of habit, with little conscience. Such a person will erode the foundation of trust in a relationship.

The lying may have started when he was a child to avoid punishment and escalated to lying to impress people, or to feel accepted as he grew older. As he continued to fool people, at least in his mind, it became a habit that worked for him. Why stop when it kept him out of trouble and gave him greater status? Soon, lying spilled over into everyday, little things. He stopped trying to tell the truth. Everything became negotiable. When in a relationship with such a person, you have nothing solid on which to build. Security is absent in such a relationship. Don't bring that kind of darkness on yourself.

Jerry was a very personable guy. He was just what Gina was looking for—cute, athletic, and hard-working. Jerry met Gina in his sophomore year at the local university. He swept her off her feet with expensive dinners, gifts, and romantic gestures. She also enjoyed his quick wit and charming personality. But after dating for about six weeks, she noticed several discrepancies in his stories.

He had talked about being a star high school basketball player with MVP trophies, which enabled him to get a full scholarship for college. He claimed his family was quite wealthy, that he had come from generations of money. Jerry had also implied he was an A student—getting the top grades in the class and making the other students jealous. He bragged about all the great things teachers had said about him in front of the class.

As Gina spent more time with Jerry, she realized some of his stories didn't add up. She saw his high school senior year book—he was listed as second string on the basketball team. She met his mom and dad on a visit over Thanksgiving, and they were driving an old car and talked about some major home repairs they couldn't afford. And Gina accidentally saw Jerry's grades lying on his desk. He had 3 C's, 2 B's, and 1 D. If he had told her the truth, she wouldn't have cared about any of those things. Now she wasn't sure what she should do.

She began doubting his far-fetched stories of heroism and bravery. When she asked him about those incidents, he changed some of the basic details—when, where, and how. Now she knew that he hadn't saved a child from a burning house or rescued drowning dogs in a flood. He hadn't received special recognition from the governor nor had a street named after him in his hometown.

While lying to impress was bad enough, she discovered that it was much more than that. Several times when Jerry had told Gina he'd spend the evening with her, he'd call at the last minute and say he was in the library finishing a big project or paper. One time she felt sorry for him and decided to take him a snack, because he was going to miss dinner. She looked throughout the library for him, but didn't find him. Gina never confronted him because she didn't want him to think she was checking up on him. At the time she assumed there was a good explanation, so she gave him the benefit of the doubt. Later she found he'd gone to a church meeting with a friend.

Another time Jerry had cancelled with her because he had "a paper due the next day." She discovered he had been at a party. Their mutual friend, Kim, asked Gina if she was feeling better. Jerry had told Kim that Gina had missed the party because she was sick. Kim also mentioned he had another girl with him who was "just a friend."

Lots of other things started to fall into place when Gina was willing to doubt small inconsequential things he'd told her. He was actually a junk-food fanatic, not a health-food nut. That explained all the wrappers in his car that were supposed to belong to his friends, and it explained why they didn't eat many meals together. When Gina thought about Jerry lying about such silly things, it made her realize she really didn't know him at all. Was he lying about how he felt about her?

Gina soon discovered that Jerry's dishonesty was also bringing major consequences into his life. Shay, Gina's friend, was in Jerry's class and had overheard the professor talking to him about his plagiarized paper. At first Jerry had denied it, but when the professor showed him proof, he admitted that he had waited until the last minute to write the paper and had run out of time, so he downloaded a paper off the Internet. The professor had consulted the dean, and Jerry was on academic probation. If he committed any other offense, he would be forced to leave the university.

Jerry also had lied to his bank about his debit card, saying it had been stolen and someone else had used it. She heard him telling the fraud department that the charges on a certain date from the county fair were not his, but she knew they were because she had been with him at the fair that day. At that point, Gina realized she had gone as far as she could in the relationship. She couldn't trust anything Jerry told her, and she knew that he could end up in prison for fraud if he continued down the road he was on. She wisely broke it off. A compulsive liar is an impossible match for a good relationship.

Alert: Risk

To Leave or Not to Leave

If any of the above situations sound familiar, ask God for wisdom and insight and to help you to be honest with yourself. You must decide when a relationship is not going to work and is causing you soul toll. When this occurs, be courageous and get on with your life. It is not easy, especially if you have been in a relationship with the person a long time or genuinely love him and have been hoping and praying for change. Only you know when problems have been confronted and remain unresolved, and only you know the full effect he is having on you and possibly on your family as well. If you are uncertain, talk to clergy or a counselor for help with the decision. Don't put it off another day.

Many people feel they will never find someone who loves them as much and that they will never love anyone as much as the person they are dating. Others fall for the "something is better than nothing" lie. Don't be deceived by these lies. While we are made for relationship and closeness, a bad relationship filled with any of the unresolved "viruses" listed above will likely bring more damage than health to your life. Don't believe the lie that you'll never find anyone else. You are a lovable creation of your creator God, and you can find love again, but not until you move on and leave a bad situation behind. If you are married and find one of these viruses has brought sickness to your relationship, seek the help of counselors or clergy to help in the situation.

3

Spark to Flame

Where Is the Spark?

Love is much more than warm, fuzzy feelings. Unfortunately, today's culture is obsessed with the feeling of love. I often hear, "I don't love him anymore." The giddy feeling of being in love is gone, so they believe the relationship is over. Yes, warm feelings toward our spouse are important and can be rekindled, but they should not be confused with true love. If the relationship has turned platonic, it needs a tune up, not a new engine.

I recently talked with Jacob, who had been married several years to an incredible woman, Kyra. She was everything he had ever dreamed of: beautiful, ambitious, intelligent, a wonderful mother, and a great cook. He said she was his best friend, the nicest person you could ever meet. But they had "grown apart." They each had successful careers and were making good money, so that was not an issue. While they were both wonderful people with good intentions, they hadn't nurtured or "fed" their relationship.

Jacob felt like a failure when he saw couples who were obviously in love, and he felt he couldn't make Kyra happy. He believed he wasn't right for her, so he finally asked Kyra for a divorce. He told her that he wanted her to be happy. She was shocked. While she knew they had lost something, she still thought they had a fairly good relationship. Often this is the case. Only one person believes the relationship is unworkable, but doesn't talk about it until he or she is ready to exit. The other is clueless about his or her feelings.

Jacob had let minor disappointments and changes in their lives become insurmountable barriers. Kyra didn't wait up for him when he worked late as she had in the early years of their marriage. She seemed preoccupied with the kids most of the time and didn't seem to have time for him. He felt less important to her. And Jacob couldn't remember the last time they had made love—three or four months at least. Often Kyra's job required her to work weekends, which left Jacob to plan and execute family activities by himself. He never mentioned these disappointments because he felt Kyra was genuinely a good person. How could he complain? Instead, he let these small things rob him of his warm feelings toward her and reasoned they must not be right for each other. None of the things that bothered him were moral issues. But they were things over which Jacob had taken offense, but never brought up. Because he hadn't communicated these things to Kyra, she had little idea of what bothered him or why their feelings had cooled.

Jacob also had contributed to the demise of romantic feelings. He frequently complimented other women in her presence, but he never complimented Kyra. He was always working—checking voicemail, e-mail, and returning calls, even when involved in family activities. Many times when Kyra disciplined the children, he contradicted her, thus undermining her authority. He often handled his anger toward Kyra passive aggressively because he hadn't dealt with his disappointments directly. He bought her gifts that he knew she wouldn't like and for special occasions chose restaurants she disliked. Of course, she didn't mention these offenses because, after all, he was doing something "nice" for her. All of these actions led to her feeling less romantic toward him. It was a downward cycle they perpetuated.

Obviously, both Jason and Kyra could make changes that would encourage those romantic feelings to return. But one of them would have to take the initiative and stick with it, even if he or she didn't see any immediate change. It takes time to refocus the direction of a relationship. Often it has taken years to arrive at its current destination and will take some time to move to a better place.

The romantic tone for the marriage is usually set by the husband. That is somewhat ironic, because women are generally more emotional and sensitive, but women are typically the responders. Now before you label me sexist, let me say that either party can attempt to bring the spark back into the relationship by taking some of the following steps, but it is almost always successful when initiated by the male. If these things have no effect, there may be deeper issues or resentments that need to be resolved. Seek the help of wise clergy or a counselor.

Recipe for "Spark" (For Married Couples and Hopefuls)

Often it is the little things that bring about damage in a relationship. If the feelings have faded, try some of the following tips for rekindling the sparks. They take some effort, but not as much as you might expect. The natural order is for things to decline without attention—scientists call this phenomenon entropy. What would happen if you ignored the routine maintenance of your home? Where we live, by the southern coast, regular maintenance includes periodic bug control, cleaning outside mildew with a pressure washer, replacing lights, cutting the grass, weed-eating, sweeping sand off of the porches, cleaning the carpets and tile, dusting, and deep-cleaning bathrooms and kitchens. Without care, the home would be overrun with bugs, mildew, dirt, sand, and germs. Not a very inviting picture. Those who are married have been entrusted with a precious relationship. Surely we should care more about our relationship than about our home, so make the effort to nurture it. Fight emotional entropy.

Weekly Date Night

Weekly, take time for the two of you to do something you both enjoy. It doesn't have to be expensive. Find a variety of things to do—a movie, dinner, dessert, Starbucks, a concert, mini golf, hiking, biking, the museum, theater, shopping, dancing or a walk on the beach—whatever you both enjoy. During your date, don't carry on extended conversations on your cell phone, and don't check e-mail while you wait for dinner to be served. Leave your cell phone in the car, and devote your time to your spouse. Do make your true love feel he or she is the most important person in the world—that this time is just for the two of you.

Reserve "Talk Time" Every Day

Depending on when you are both available and when you will be least interrupted and distracted, carve out at least fifteen minutes a day to catch up with what is going on in each other's lives. Just knowing that another person loves you enough to want to know about your thoughts, your feelings, and your day will feed the spark. That's especially true for women. Don't always talk about surface issues, but allow the conversation to wander into the realm of feelings, hopes, and dreams. Ask each other deeper questions. Let this time be a positive building time for the relationship.

Limit Negative Talks for Private Times

Don't ever bring up something negative about your honey in front of the kids or other family members or friends. While you may have valid complaints, the following biblical advice is effective for maintaining respect and goodwill. "If your brother sins against you, go and show him his fault, just between the two of you" (Matt. 18:15). While it is important and necessary to bring up issues that bother us, it is embarrassing for the person being "criticized" and demonstrates a lack of respect. None of us wants to feel put down by the person closest to us in front of others. And most people don't want to engage in such a discussion in public. Show respect by talking privately.

Focus on the Positive

"Whatever is true, whatever is noble, whatever is right, whatever is pure, whatever is lovely, whatever is admirable—if anything is excellent or praiseworthy—think about such things." (Phil. 4:8)

Rarely does anyone marry someone he or she can't stand. We were drawn to our mate because he or she had many qualities we loved—his humor, intelligence, kindness, or panache; her fun-loving spirit, stability, attractiveness, or sensitivity. We must never let our focus remain on the small irritations that will come in any relationship, but we must focus on all of the great positive attributes of our love. And we need to let our spouse know on a regular basis how much we appreciate his or her _____. Fill in the blank regularly with different qualities. While men may be tempted to focus on a woman's physical attributes—especially if she is attractive, a woman also appreciates hearing positive encouragements about her soul.

Listen

"Everyone should be quick to listen, slow to speak, and slow to become angry." (James 1:9)

In our busy lives it is easy to try to multi-task our families. We are cooking dinner, watching the news, helping the kids with homework, and checking e-mail from work. Sometimes important things are being said, and we are not really hearing the message. We either miss the content altogether, or we don't really understand the intent.

When we truly listen to not just the words, but to the message behind the words, we are taking the time to give of ourselves. Not everyone can read between the lines, and there is danger in jumping to conclusions when listening, but if you listen carefully, you will hear the heart of the speaker. Try to make eye contact, nod, give verbal cues, and when not sure what the speaker means, ask for clarification. What is motivating her, what concerns her, what are her dreams, what are her priorities? We will feel closer to someone when we truly listen.

Some advocate repeating back what you think a person is saying to make sure you really understand, but if overdone that can become irritating and stifle real conversation. Don't worry if you don't catch every slight innuendo. If you feel you need clarification, don't be afraid to ask for it. Who doesn't want to be understood? While we all have many similarities, we are also all different. Listening and learning about another soul is a challenge, but it can bring great satisfaction.

Cuddle

Show affection to your mate in a way that he appreciates. If it means rubbing his back and neck or his feet to accommodate his wishes, do it. Hold hands, put your arms around each other, or walk arm in arm in the mall. While watching TV or eating dinner, reach over and touch his arm or hand. If one or both of you have enjoyed any of these gestures in the past, you can encourage the spark by engaging them again. Physical touch encourages bonding on an emotional level. It is not hypocritical to do these things even if you don't feel "in love." Touching will let your mate know of your love, of your choosing to love him. Often such gestures of tenderness will warm his heart and yours.

Gifts and Surprises

Most of us enjoy receiving gifts. By spending time talking with your mate, dating her and actively listening, you may have a better idea of a gift she would enjoy. Don't choose something for the house or that you would enjoy. Make sure it is something that she will genuinely appreciate. If you love yellow, but your spouse doesn't care for it, don't buy her a yellow sweater because you fell in love with it. Don't buy her the new CD you have been wanting or get a dog if she loves cats. If she loves biographies, buy her a biography, not a mystery that you would enjoy. A little common sense goes a long way when buying gifts.

If you are still uncertain, most women enjoy flowers, perfume, jewelry or a weekend away as gifts, because these things are associated with romance. But not all women want these things. Some would rather have a nice jacket or a new laptop. Most men appreciate romantic gifts of cologne, a wallet, a watch, or clothing. Anything personal is usually more romantic. But your man may prefer tickets to the game or a new grill. By spending time with your spouse, you will have a deeper understanding of his or her tastes and desires. If you are still lost for a gift, you can ask her for some ideas and choose one. She will appreciate that you made the effort to buy something she wanted.

Another way to develop the spark is to leave each other surprises. Notes, e-mails, or messages at unexpected times in unexpected places let her know you love her and think about her. When my husband travels, he often leaves me notes on index cards in unexpected places around the house. I love it. Everyone enjoys knowing they are being thought about.

Love Is Sacrifice

"This is how we know what love is: Jesus Christ laid down his life for us. And we ought to lay down our lives for our brothers." (1 John 3:16)

True love is sacrifice. Don't marry someone for whom you are not willing to sacrifice. Don't marry her unless she is willing to sacrifice for you. Marriage is 100 percent/100 percent, not 50 percent/50 percent. I'm not advocating being a doormat, but if your spouse-to-be feels strongly about something, are you willing to give up what you want for her, and is she willing to give up what she wants when you feel strongly about something? If so, you will have no trouble compromising to make each other happy. Of course, you will let each other down at times and not give 100 percent. But when your partner isn't giving her all, it is not the time to pull back and do likewise. It is time to continue to give all you have in order to make the relationship the best it can be. That kind of love is an upward spiral, drawing the person toward you rather than pushing her away.

SECTION I: RELATIONSHIP REALITIES

OVERVIEW

Summary

Our hearts should be protected by setting up guidelines before we commit to a serious relationship. Wait a full year before becoming engaged. Observe your potential spouse with his family to see if he interacts with his family as he does with you. Realize that finding a serious relationship is not a panacea; you must be satisfied prior to finding "the one." Don't expect the person to change; if you don't want him the way he is, then don't commit. Opposites often attract and can be successful if aware of potential pitfalls. Find someone with whom you can be spiritually yoked and attend Christian pre-marriage counseling.

Pay attention to "virus alerts:" nagging feelings, warnings from friends and family, control issues, addictions, mood swings, violence/abuse, extreme selfishness/pride, neediness, and compulsive lying. All of these are reasons to stop moving forward until there is an authentic, lasting change.

Every relationship goes through cycles of emotions. Some feel the relationship should be built on romantic feelings. While this is paramount in our culture, it is not true biblical love. Warm feelings toward our spouse are certainly healthy and appropriate and should be nurtured, but not used for a measure of love. Tips are given for rekindling the spark. But, actually, love's true foundation is sacrifice.

Light Reality

• Password-protect your heart. Decide you will not give it away before you determine that the relationship is healthy.
• Knowing how to judge a relationship objectively will enable you to move beyond the pull of the heart to wisely choose the most important relationship of your life.

- While assessing the relationship, certain risks should cause you to stop short. These concerns should be deal breakers unless the person is seeking help and exhibits different behavior over a long period of time.
- Like everything else in life, a relationship must be nurtured and protected to grow and be healthy.
- If already married, but in an unhealthy relationship, taking appropriate action will bring about positive changes.

Dark Reality

- When we join our heart to an unhealthy person in a serious relationship, we open ourselves to potentially deep pain.
- Hurt inflicted by the one we expect will love us unconditionally can cause lasting scars and possibly hinder future relationships.
- An unhealthy relationship may produce feelings of betrayal, anger, rage, disappointment, discouragement, depression, entrapment, or disillusionment.
- Inaction in an unhealthy relationship leads to further deterioration and enablement.
- With appropriate processing, these heartbreaks can heal over time, but if they are ongoing, they will obstruct your wellspring of life, making it a trickle rather than a flood.

Reality Discussion Questions

1. Am I in any kind of denial about my significant relationships?

_____

_____

2. Are there any viruses invading my relationship with the person I am dating or to whom I am married?

_____

_____

3. If so, what can I do to address this/these issue/s?

_____

_____

4. What attracted me to my spouse or potential spouse?

_____

_____

5. How can I show gratefulness for these and other good qualities he or she possesses in a way he or she will appreciate?

_____

_____

6. What am I doing to nurture my relationship?

_____

_____

7. What more can I do?

_____

_____

8. Retake the quiz at the beginning of Relationship Realities. Did you change any of your answers? Which ones and why?

_____

_____

Prayer

Heavenly Father, thank you for the people you have allowed in my life. Help me to be wise in my choice of significant relationships and seek to follow your wisdom. I know you desire my closest relationships to reflect the love you have for me, so help me to learn to love as you do. May I see the importance of nurturing my most important relationships and have the wisdom to do so in ways that they will feel loved. Let your love, love through me. In Jesus' name, amen.

SECTION II: REALITIES OF GOD'S WILL

Quiz

Multiple Choice Stories

Choose the *best* answer to the questions below.

1. You have been looking for a job for three months after you graduate and are anxious to get on with your life. Your fifty applications yield nine job interviews and three job offers. At job number one, the company is paying way below what you were hoping for, but it seems like a fun and relaxed place to work. Job number two is paying what you had hoped to earn, but the company seems a little unstable. They are small, have been in business for less than a year, and have mixed reviews from customers. You are concerned that they may not be in business for long. Job number three is paying less than the new company, but is more stable. They have a good review with their clients and are large enough that you could expect to be promoted over time if you do well. They have frequent job reviews and quotas, so you know it would have more stress than job number one. But if you accept job number one, you'll have to continue to live with your parents, at least for awhile. If you take either of the other two jobs, you'll be able to move out on your own—something you'd rather do sooner than later. You pray about it, but don't seem to have any clear direction.

You should _____.

  a. not do anything. Continue to search for a different job until you have clear direction from God.

  b. thank God for the three open doors and choose the most practical one—job number three. You will have a fighting chance to survive on the pay and will be able to look forward to greater opportunities in the future.

c. thank God for the three open doors and take job number two since it pays the most. Even if it only lasts for a short time, you will be ahead financially and be able to get your student loans paid down. You'll gain experience in your field and more easily find a job if the company doesn't make it. It is the expedient decision.

d. take job number one. You believe God wants you to be happy, and believe you would be most content in this position because there would be the least amount of stress. You will have to continue to live with your parents until you can save up enough to move out on your own.

2. You have been dating Chris for about three months when he announces that he feels it is God's will that you get married. He seems to be a very spiritual person—reads his Bible every morning and never misses church. You have been very busy with school and work and haven't had as much time to seek God. The relationship has gone smoothly, but you haven't spent a lot of time together because of your schedules, although you do talk on the phone and text every day. You are crazy about him, but don't know if you are ready to make a marriage commitment. You haven't met any of his family or friends from his home in Chicago and feel that you don't know him well.

You should _____.

a. tell him you'd like to meet his family before you make such a big commitment, and if all goes well, proceed.

b. break up with him. He is surely a quack to think God would tell him you should marry without telling you the same thing.

c. tell him that you are hesitant to make that kind of commitment until more time has passed. You want to date a year before getting engaged.

    d.   marry him. You don't see any red flags and you love him; there is no reason to wait.

3.   Your good friend Amanda has had a horrible year. She was not able to graduate with your class because she was in the hospital for over two months during fall semester. She is fully recovered now, but sad to see her friends going back home or on to great jobs around the country. Another setback Amanda suffered is a shortfall in funds for her final semester. Her parents had her college tuition invested in stocks that plunged. And recently an ice storm hit, and she has been without electricity for a week. To top it all off, her beloved dog, Angel, died. Amanda tells you she is overwhelmed and discouraged. She feels like God is punishing her. She thinks she must have done something wrong, but has no idea what. She believes if she were in God's will, life would be trouble-free.

You should _____.

    a.   encourage her to examine her heart for sin that is bringing all of this misfortune upon her. You agree that if she were in God's will, everything would be going smoothly.

    b.   encourage her to see all of the good things she has going on in her life. Remind her that everyone has bad things happen to them, some more at one time than another, but it doesn't indicate that God is angry with her.

    c.   tell her to start doing good things for everyone around her. This should make up for her bad karma and get her back in God's good graces.

    d.   encourage her to forget about God if that is the way he is going to treat her. If her devotion doesn't bring about a better life, then what is the point? She shouldn't waste her time.

TRUE OR FALSE?

Realities of God's Will

True/False 1. Because God's will is a serious matter, you should wrestle over every decision until you know you are following God's perfect plan for you.

True/False 2. Following God's will means never choosing what you want.

True/False 3. Finding God's primary will for your life involves where you live, the person you marry, and what job you hold.

True/False 4. When we are in God's will, we will encounter few obstacles.

True/False 5. When we are in God's will, we will see God do miraculous things for us.

True/False 6. There is one person in the world God has chosen for each of us to marry.

True/False 7. You find God's will primarily at critical turning points in your life.

True/False 8. If we make a poor choice, good can still come out of it.

True/False 9. Asking what Jesus would do is the best method for determining God's will.

True/False 10. The best analogy of being in God's will is allowing him to pull the strings, like a puppeteer.

4

Traps to Avoid

In the church today thousands, if not millions, of individuals sincerely want to find God's will for their lives. They are under the impression that God has a very specific "time-and-place" plan for their life, or for "the one" to marry. Often these plans seem to be elusive mysteries cloaked in darkness. Some people fear being out of God's "perfect" will and agonize to the point of despair trying to discover God's specific plan at any given time. When I was in my twenties, I felt God's will was for me to find an extremely specific job in a specific place; I didn't grasp the broader implications of God's will. This struggle is not uncommon. Rather than being encouraged or inspired, many become disillusioned or disheartened trying to figure out God's "perfect" plan for their life.

Traps Concerning God's Will

Despondency and Confusion
While teaching in a Bible College several years ago, one of my students, John, was seeking God's will regarding his choice of a wife. John was a great student. He always came to class prepared and often turned in assignments before they were due. He was a little shy, but very intelligent and personable, a really nice guy. One day I heard that John had committed suicide; I was stunned. I learned that he had become very depressed trying to discover God's will in regard to a girl he had met at church. He didn't want to fail God and marry her if she was not "God's will" for him. He agonized for months over this decision, and when he finally could not

discern God's will one way or the other, he became deeply depressed and eventually took his own life. This is a tragic, extreme case, but the confusion and uncertainty is reflected to a lesser extent in the lives of thousands who have sincerely wanted to be in God's will.

Chapter 5, *Uncloaking the Mystery,* will explain that God's will is not a deeply hidden secret that only the super-spiritual can discern, but is clearly explained in Scripture.

Confusing Our Will with God's

Another potential trap in emphasizing a specific time and place as God's primary will is to falsely attribute our choices as God's will. We see signs everywhere that God is calling us to a person or place when, in fact, those signs may actually be our plans or desires. It is fine to plan, as long as we submit our plans to God and are willing to change course, if necessary.

Gary worked for me several years ago and wanted to move to a warmer climate for health reasons. But rather than saying he was moving because of health concerns, he felt he couldn't make a move without God leading him. Consequently, he saw signs everywhere that the move was God's will. So he sold his home, auctioned his furniture and everything he had, and moved without securing another job or place to live. He had a hard time finding work, housing was very expensive, and he had difficulty adjusting to the cultural differences in the area. Within a year he had to admit that God probably hadn't led him to move. He had confused his will with God's.

It was not wrong for him to want to move to a warmer climate to improve his health. But because he had confused God's will with his will, he bypassed normal planning—visiting the area, securing adequate affordable housing, finding work that he liked, and basically evaluating the move from a practical standpoint. Instead, he turned the move into a spiritual decision based on God's leading and anticipated supernatural provision. When the move proved to be unproductive, he was disillusioned and returned to the area from which he had moved with most of his savings gone. He was sincerely wrong and paid a hefty price.

Had Gary admitted that he wanted to move to a warmer climate for health reasons, he might have researched several areas of the country, made a few visits, investigated housing and jobs more thoroughly, and made a move that was more practical. Instead he locked into one particular place as God's leading and hastily made a poor decision thinking it would all work out because it was "God's will."

Logical, well-thought-out, practical decisions are not wrong. It does not indicate a lack of trust in God, but shows we are using the minds he has given us. "Make plans by seeking advice" (Prov. 20:18a). "An upright man gives thought to his ways" (Prov. 21:29b). Preparing for the future shows responsibility. Jesus said, "Suppose one of you wants to build a tower. Will he not first sit down and estimate the cost to see if he has enough money to complete it?" (Luke 14:28). Planning ahead is wise and can prevent drifting onto a dark path.

Believing if We are In God's Will, Life will Be Easy

Finding God's primary will for our life is easy and clearly explained in Scripture, but following God's will is not always easy. In the church there is often a misconception that if we are in God's will and living right, life will just fall into place, and if we are out of God's perfect place for us, we'll have turmoil. The truth is that life, at times, falls into place for both believers and unbelievers. And life also throws all of us curveballs—illness, unemployment, relationship challenges, or rising food and gas prices. None of these are pleasant, but they are common to all. If you are human, you will suffer to some extent—in or out of God's will. But you can have confidence that the more closely you follow God's way of life, the less self-imposed suffering and soul toll you'll endure.

A dichotomy exists in the lives of the heroes of the faith found in Hebrews 11. Everyone in this chapter is commended for his or her faith and following God. Yet they had vastly different experiences that proved their faith. Some were victorious in this life, some suffered in this life, and some were victorious at times and suffered at other times.

On the positive side, Enoch never saw death. Noah was saved from the flood, Abraham and Sarah had a son in their old age, Moses saw God intervene by saving his people in the Passover and the Red Sea, Joshua saw Jericho fall, others conquered kingdoms, shut the mouths of lions, quenched the fury of flames, escaped the sword, routed foreign enemies, and certain women received back those who had died. If one didn't read the entire chapter, you might conclude that if you are in God's will, everything will work out fine—you will be victorious.

In order to maintain an accurate picture, we must also acknowledge the negative circumstances in which many faithful found themselves, as seen in the rest of the chapter. Abraham and his family lived in tents, rather than a permanent city. Moses was first mistreated with the people of God before he saw miraculous interventions. Many believers were tortured, flogged, chained, imprisoned, stoned, sawed in two, put to death by the sword, destitute, persecuted, mistreated, wandered in deserts, mountains, caves and holes in the ground. Not our definition of victory.

In Hebrews 11, God commends all of these people for their faith and says they were looking forward to a heavenly city whose architect and builder is God. They did not all receive deliverance on this earth. Some saw both miracles and suffering. But all of them believed that God exists, and that he rewards those who seek him, sometimes in this life and always in the life to come. They will all be rewarded, whether they saw prosperity or pain in this life. And there is some indication that those who suffered for being a Christian in this life will gain a greater reward in the life to come. How foolish we are to condemn those who have trouble in this life as being out of God's will.

5

Uncloaking the Mystery

God's Primary Will for Us Is Spiritual

While not wanting to minimize the reality of God's intimate involvement in our lives, his greatest will for us is not in where we live, the job we hold, or the person we marry—though these are important decisions. His greatest will for us is spiritual transformation. "Do not conform any longer to the pattern of this world, but be transformed by the renewing of your mind. Then you will be able to test and approve what God's will is—his good, pleasing and perfect will" (Rom. 12:2).

God's perfect will is for us to be transformed by truth into the image of Christ, not physically, but spiritually. This transformation is a lifelong process. We all start life self-centered and self-honoring, born with a sin nature. If we are Christians, God works in us to transform our lives into those that are other-centered and God-honoring—like the life of Jesus. Of course, we must also consider our own needs and take care of ourselves. If we are going to love others as we love ourselves, we must attend to ourselves. God loves us as much as those he wants us to love. As we learn and apply the truth of Scripture, our lives will be transformed more and more for as long as we live. "And we, who with unveiled faces all reflect the Lord's glory, are being transformed into his likeness with ever-increasing glory, which comes from the Lord, who is the Spirit" (2 Cor. 3:18).

In Ephesians 5 Paul tells Christians to understand what the will of God is. The chapter instructs us to imitate God, live a life of love, avoid sexual immorality, give thanks, live in the light in righteousness, goodness and truth, live wisely, avoid drunkenness, be filled with the spirit, sing in our hearts to God, and submit to each other. These, again, are spiritual instructions for knowing and living in God's will. When we follow these spiritual instructions, we are following God's will. As we grow in grace and truth, we are in God's will. God's will is not a great, deeply cloaked mystery. It is easy to know God's primary will for our lives.

God has explained his will clearly for us in his word. He wants our hearts, minds, and spirits to be right. Our physical address is secondary. Wherever we are, we can do good, we can love, and we can walk in the light. Physical, emotional, and spiritual need is present everywhere in the world—some places more than others—but need is everywhere. So don't despair; wherever you are, you can be in God's will, loving those around you, growing in your understanding of him and his grace in your life. His primary concern is that we are conformed more and more into his image and glorify him.

The WWJD craze had the right idea, but often faulty execution. The concept is that, in any particular situation, I can ask myself, "What would Jesus do," and then act accordingly. In theory this is an awesome guide for living. The breakdown comes when we don't know what he would do because we don't know him well enough. I have heard a number of Christians espouse what they thought Jesus would do in a situation—and honestly it didn't sound anything like what Jesus would do, but a lot like what they would do! To understand what he would do, you must "let the word of Christ dwell in you richly" (Col. 3:16). Only when we know him well, will we know what he would do.

An additional obstacle for knowing what Jesus would do is our modern culture. It is very different today than when Jesus walked the earth, so even when we do know him well, we often need to pray for wisdom and seek council to assess what is the right and Christ-like response. God sees our hearts, so we can have confidence that even if we inadvertently make a less-than-perfect choice, God is able to use our right spirit and bring good out of every situation.

God's Will Is that All Will Be Saved

God wants everyone to be saved and come to a knowledge of the truth (1 Tim. 2:4). He loves us and has clearly provided the means through Jesus for a restored relationship with him. The death of Christ was for everyone, but only those who accept his gift of salvation will be saved. When we realize we can't ever be good enough or earn our salvation, but that Jesus paid for our sin on the cross, we can gratefully accept his forgiveness and be restored to a relationship with God. If the whole world followed God's will, everyone would be in a loving relationship with him. That is his highest desire for every person.

Lord Willing

Another sense in which God's will is used in Scripture is submission to the humbling knowledge that our very life is dependent on him. We cannot presume that we will accomplish this or that. We do not even know if we have tomorrow. God has ultimate control, and if he chooses to intervene, our lives could take a significant change in direction. Several passages refer to God's will in this sense.

The best example and explanation of this use of God's will is found in James 4:13–16, "Now listen, you who say, 'Today or tomorrow we will go to this or that city, spend a year there, carry on business and make money.' Why, you do not even know what will happen tomorrow. What is your life? You are a mist that appears for a little while and then vanishes. Instead, you ought to say, 'If it is the Lord's will, we will live and do this or that.' As it is, you boast and brag. All such boasting is evil."

Acknowledging God's will in this sense is merely an acknowledgment that he is God, the creator, and we are his creation. We are truly dependent on him for everything. Adopting this attitude displays our humility. God has supreme power and authority; we are not able to know what our future holds with absolute certainty. We can plan, but we must acknowledge that God is the ultimate source of all life and fulfillment of our plans.

6

Individual Leading

Plan and Submit

God does not take offense at our planning as long as we understand and submit our plans to his ultimate authority. "In his heart a man plans his course, but the Lord determines his steps" (Prov. 16:9). God is God. He can intervene and arrange anything in our life. If we love him, we know he will work everything for our good—even things that are the result of a sin-tainted world.

God is not against us, nor does he want to manipulate our every move. He desires that we walk in his ways, loving him and others. He is ultimately in control and will often make our plans succeed: "May he give you the desire of your heart and make all your plans succeed" (Ps. 20:4). He wants us to live freely, not bound by a false concept of his will, feeling we have only one narrow path of daily choices to stay in his will. He doesn't want us to agonize at every turn. If our spirits are right, he will open doors for us to do good, love and be loved, glorify him, and grow more and more into his image. This is the light path of success.

God's Call to a Mission

While God's greatest will is for all people to come to a saving knowledge of him and be conformed into his image, he also sometimes leads a person in a particular direction. I do not discount that possibility or its importance when God requires something specific of you. In the burning bush, God spoke to Moses about leading his people out of captivity; he told Jonah to preach to the people of Nineveh; he asked Noah to build an ark; in a dream he directed Joseph to flee to Egypt with baby Jesus; he led Jesus into the desert to be tempted; and in a vision he called Paul to go to Macedonia. Scripture is filled with examples of God's specific leading to accomplish specific goals. While these individuals were already in God's will, following his ways, they were called to a specific mission.

In the book of Esther, Mordecai encourages Queen Esther to approach the king to ask for deliverance from an edict that would destroy the Jews. He wisely states, "For if you remain silent at this time, relief and deliverance for the Jews will arise from another place" (Esther 4:14). Mordecai believed Esther was in place for their deliverance, but he also knew that if she did not fulfill this specific mission, God would raise another to fulfill his purposes. God does not need us; he is God. He is much greater than our decisions. If God calls you to a specific mission, humbly accept it and know he will be with you even when the way is hard or filled with obstacles. To be chosen to work for him is an honor.

While sometimes sacrifices are required to follow God's leading to a particular place, a physical move is often easier than following after God's heart. A physical change of address may require physical sacrifices, as well as some emotional ones—being away from family and friends, etc. They are real sacrifices for which God promises to reward (Mark 10:29–30). But God's leading in our hearts can be even more challenging. We must face our sins and shortcomings. God may ask us to confess and repent of a sin. That takes humility, honesty, and dependence on Him. It involves willingness to die to ourselves and live for God.

God's will always draws us deeper into his relational wisdom. His still, small voice may say, "Be kind, even though they are unkind," "Vengeance is mine, don't retaliate," "Do this small good deed in my name," "Hold your tongue," "Yes, you are gifted, but don't become arrogant. Remember who gave you your talents," "Speak the truth in love," "You were wrong, ask for forgiveness," or "Reach out to that lonely person." Much of God's deeper, higher, greater will in our lives is the spiritual leading that results in our spiritual growth and maturity. You do not need to have a seminary degree to know God's will, but you must be a willing servant.

Right Place, Wrong Heart

It is possible to be where God wants you to be geographically, but be out of his will. Moses led the Israelites from captivity in Egypt into the desert. They were in God's perfect geographical plan. They had seen miraculous signs and wonders in their deliverance, yet refused to believe God. The Israelites were unfaithful, creating a golden calf to worship. Scripture says they treated God with contempt and grumbled against him, wanting to go back to Egypt. Because they were out of God's primary will, having an unbelieving heart, it didn't matter that they were in his physical will. Only Joshua and Caleb, who had stayed faithful to God's will spiritually (Num. 14), were allowed into the Promised Land. His higher, greater will for us is spiritual. Be more concerned with your heart than with your address.

When we are walking in God's will, following his ways—loving God, doing good, loving others, and walking on the light path—he may call us to a specific mission. Most of the time, when God called his servants to specific tasks, they were already walking in his will. God's request for a specific action was followed by either obedience or disobedience. If someone chooses to disobey when they have received a specific mission from God, they may suffer consequences, as did Jonah, who ended up in the belly of a big fish, and as did the Israelites who died in the desert, never entering the Promised Land flowing with milk and honey. The Israelites missed out. Although their address was in God's will, their hearts were wrong.

Brad grew up in church and became a believer in his early teens. As he thought about the direction for his life, he decided to follow in his retired grandfather's footsteps and go to a university where he could study the Bible and ministry. His grandpa had been a country preacher for years, and Brad thought he would enjoy being in charge of a church. As he progressed through his program, he took a position as a youth pastor and began activities for the Junior High and High School kids. Since his grandpa had served in that church for five decades, Brad felt entitled to his position. He didn't consider it an honor or feel the true weight of his responsibility.

Brad gradually became more and more harsh with the students. He didn't exercise any mercy or grace toward them, only the letter of the law. Parents soon began to complain, and Brad was called in before the senior pastor. Brad didn't understand. He felt he was fulfilling God's will for his life. He'd not opted for a lucrative career like many of his friends, and he was making sacrifices for the ministry. How could he be out of God's will when he was in a Christian university and working in youth ministry? He had focused so much on what he would do, he hadn't been careful about his own spiritual condition. He was moving in a godly direction, but he hadn't allowed God to work in his heart. In order to truly be where God wanted him, he needed to be who God wanted him to be. Not that he needed to be perfect, but he needed to be moving forward spiritually and open to God's spiritual leading. Spiritual transformation is God's primary, ultimate will for our lives.

God's Will and Marriage

Many sincere people have declared it is God's will for them to marry a particular person. I know several people who believe God told them to marry John or Jane, but, interestingly, he didn't tell John or Jane the same thing. A few times I've seen couples marry based on this "revelation," and the results were disastrous. So what does God's word say about choosing someone to marry?

Marriage is one of the greatest decisions we make in life; it has far-reaching consequences, and it affects most decisions that follow. Without minimizing God's involvement, it is important to understand that God has allowed us options in this matter. Paul discusses the issue of marriage, saying that those who are married have to concern themselves with their spouse and won't have as much to give in devotion to God. His personal recommendation is to stay single, but clearly Paul does not condemn marriage as wrong. "If . . . he feels he ought to marry, he should do as he wants. He is not sinning. They should get married. But the man who has settled the matter in his own mind, who is under no compulsion but has control over his own will, and who has made up his mind not to marry the virgin—this man also does the right thing." (1 Cor. 7:36–38). Paul clearly says the man should do as he wants. He is not sinning if he marries or if he doesn't marry. God allows us the option to choose in this and many other matters.

The passage after that also indicates we may marry the person of our choice, as long as the person is a Christian. "But if her husband dies, she is free to marry anyone she wishes, but he must belong to the Lord" (1 Cor. 7:39). Paul says she is free to marry anyone she wishes, not the one person God has picked out of the whole world. Of course, there are wise and foolish choices, as with most things in life. Since this is a life-altering choice, we would do well to consult God's wisdom and guidance and the input of others who love us. Paul's one absolute here is that the person is in the Lord, a believer. We will bring much darkness upon ourselves if we ignore this absolute.

Free Will

God created man to be in relationship. The core of God's nature is relational, as seen in the Trinity—Father, Son, and Holy Spirit. He created man that he might have fellowship with him. He did not create man so he could have puppets to perform on the world's stage. If God called every shot for every decision we make, we would not have a relationship, but a dictatorship.

While God desires that His children respond to him in love and obedience to his ways, which will bring us a better life, he does not dictate every word and action. He wants us to honestly communicate our thoughts, feelings, and plans. He wants to be in fellowship with us, molding and making us into the spiritual image of Christ.

SECTION II: REALITIES OF GOD'S WILL

OVERVIEW

Summary

Misconceptions exist about God's perfect will for our lives. One is that his primary will is being at a particular job or place or finding a particular person to marry. Another is that we must always have his specific leading to make a decision in life, so we should look for signs that indicate his will. A third is that if we are in God's will, everything will just fall into place and our life will be easy.

A better understanding of God's will is following his ways as taught in Scripture: loving him and our neighbor as we love ourselves. When we, through truth, are being transformed into the image of Christ, we are achieving God's greatest and highest will for our lives and bringing him glory. At times, God may call us to a specific mission, and when he does, he will be with us even if it is difficult.

Light Reality

• Following God's will is not mysterious. His will is clearly explained throughout his word.
• We must learn his truth, put it into practice and, consequently, be transformed into his image.
• God's primary will is spiritual transformation in relationship with him.

Dark Reality

• If we focus only on the surface particulars of place, person, or mission we are to accomplish, we may miss the deeper spiritual realities of being in God's will.

• When our primary focus is on our mission, we may become conceited and self-absorbed, feeling God needs us, rather than acknowledging our humble position as his creation and servant.

• When we feel indispensable to God, pride and arrogance will darken our spiritual eyes.

Reality Discussion Questions

1. Before you read this chapter, what did you think of when you thought of God's will?

_____

_____

2. Have you ever fallen into any of the traps regarding God's will? If so, explain.

_____

_____

3. Have you accepted God's gift of salvation through Jesus? (God's ultimate will for us)

_____

_____

4. If so, how has that affected the life you live today?

_____

_____

5. When has it been hard for you to submit and accept that God is ultimately in control?

_____

_____

6. Have you ever been in the right place, but had the wrong attitude? If yes, what was the result?

_____

_____

7. Now that you realize that God's will is primarily spiritual, what will you do differently?

_____

_____

8. Retake the quiz at the beginning of Realities of God's Will. Did you change any of your answers? Which ones and why?

_____

_____

Prayer

Heavenly Father, thank you that your will is not a deeply buried mystery, but clearly displayed in your word. Help me to submit my life to your spiritual will, a life of love that you designed for me and also to any particular assignments you may have planned for me. It is an honor to be in relationship with you and to be used by you. Continue to keep me in your reality for as long as I live. In Jesus' name, amen.

SECTION III: PERSONALITY REALITIES

Quiz

Multiple Choice Stories

Choose the *best* answer to the questions below.

1. John, an exceptional English teacher, uses a variety of teaching methods to reach different types of learners. His unconventional approach keeps students engaged who might otherwise fall through the cracks. After being named "Teacher of the Year" by students at Springfield High three years in a row, he is now receiving negative feedback from the other English teachers. They feel he is too unconventional and not really effective—even if he is popular. He incorporates a lot of hands-on experience and field trips into the curriculum for students to write about. John also allows intense discussions and many opinions instead of giving the "right" answers and keeping tight control. The other English teachers have complained to the principle and asked that John be required to conform to conventional methods.

You are the principle. What should you do?

   a. You should tell John that you appreciate his popularity with the students, but his unconventional practices are causing problems among the faculty, so he should conform for the sake of peace.

   b. You believe the other faculty are jealous of John for achieving "Teacher of the Year" status again, so you should do nothing. Let them fight it out among themselves.

   c. You should tell the other English teachers you will look into their concerns. When you do, you discover John's students are scoring higher than the other students on standardized tests, so you report back to the complaining faculty. You stop their negativity with the facts. John's teaching methods are not wrong, just different.

d. You should have a meeting with all of the English teachers to discuss the issue and allow John to defend himself. This clears the air and lets everyone know they have an equal say and a right to their opinion. You encourage respect for differences among teaching styles.

e. a or b

f. c or d

2. For several semesters during college Amber interned for a large insurance company. Because they were impressed with her work ethic and creative solutions to problems, they hired her as a department manager when she graduated. Amber has stepped into a position that was held by the same person for over twenty-five years. Loyalties are strong to the former manager, and Amber is finding a lot of resistance to her new ways of doing things. Daily she hears, "We've never done it that way before." A few employees follow Amber's new guidelines, but most continue to follow the previous supervisor's "way." Productivity is down and Amber is frustrated.

You are Amber's boss and observe the discord and lack of productivity. What should you do?

a. You should institute team building exercises in Amber's department and hope for the best. You assume this will help employees bond with Amber and respect her as the new authority.

b. You should discuss the situation with Amber explaining that her rapid changes are causing conflict among those she is leading. You should encourage her to slow down until those she supervises learn to trust and respect her judgment.

c. You should encourage Amber to have open discussions with her employees explaining why she believes each change would improve the system. Ask her to request and consider her staff's input before making modifications to current procedures and policies.

d. At the next staff meeting, you should discuss chain of command and why it is important to follow the boss' lead. You should also discuss the value of supervisors holding their staff accountable.

3. Tiffany and Justin are newly married, and the differences that once attracted them are now a source of conflict. Tiffany is organized and planned. In contrast, Justin is carefree and spontaneous. Tiffany feels Justin should inform her well in advance if he is going to invite friends over, so she can have the house in tip-top shape. She also prefers to have their weekends planned in advance, so they don't end up "wasting" them. Justin enjoys living in the moment and invites his buddies over whenever he feels like it. He doesn't care if the house isn't perfect. He simply enjoys having friends around. He also prefers to leave weekends open, so he and Tiffany can do whatever they feel like doing at the time.

You are a friend to both Justin and Tiffany; they each confide in you about this personality difference that is driving them crazy. What do you do?

a. You tell Tiffany to lighten up. She should be thankful that she has such a fun-loving person in her life. She shouldn't worry about the house being perfect or their time being managed so tightly.

b. You tell Justin that he needs to grow up. He can't stay a kid all his life and live as if he were single. He is married now and should act like a responsible adult.

c. You encourage them to discuss how they feel about the issues without demeaning or accusing each other. You help them to understand each other's personality preferences and suggest possible compromises.

d. You recommend they divorce. This is an irreconcilable difference that will only get worse over time. People's basic personalities don't change.

TRUE OR FALSE?

Personality Realities

True/False 1. Most people respect others as they are, even when differences are vast.

True/False 2. For most questions in your life, black and white answers exist. There are few gray areas.

True/False 3. Assigning personality types limits our understanding of others.

True/False 4. Extroversion is not better than introversion.

True/False 5. A person who is practical and realistic will get further in life than someone who spends time dreaming about possibilities and what could be.

True/False 6. We should base our decisions on objective criteria and not emotions.

True/False 7. It is best to thoroughly research a big decision before deciding.

True/False 8. While extensive cultural differences exist, most peoples' basic motivations are the same.

True/False 9. You are who you are; there is nothing you can do about your weaknesses.

True/False 10. Not everyone is created to be used by God. You have to have a special calling and unique gifting.

7

Embrace Differences

"Just as each of us has one body with many members, and these members do not all have the same function, so in Christ we who are many form one body." (Rom. 12:4–5)

Narcissistic—Who Me?

It is human nature to have narcissistic tendencies, loving ourselves above all else. While we may acknowledge that diversity and differences are good and healthy, in actuality, we often don't live those values. To some extent we expect others to think like us, speak like us, and act like us. When they don't, we consider them "wrong." Many of these judgments take place subconsciously, but they do take place.

We mistakenly designate ourselves as the measure of what is normal and right. We want everyone else to be like us. Even subconsciously wanting others to be like us is a prideful wish. We evaluate others based on ourselves, rather than God and his objective word. "When they measure themselves by themselves and compare themselves with themselves, they are not wise" (2 Cor. 10:12).

Give God the Credit

God has created each of us with unique differences so that together we may benefit each other and his purposes in the world. These purposes include everything from the growth of individuals, to reaching the lost. So often we take credit for our talents, when in fact they are gifts from

God. Without him, we wouldn't have them. He created us and our abilities. Keeping this perspective in mind helps us avoid becoming proud and misusing our talents. It keeps us focused on glorifying him with our gifts, time, money, and all that we are.

On the flip side, if we recognize that God created us, we also must recognize that he created every other person. So when we see another person who is different from us—either superior or inferior to the way God created us—we should neither envy nor despise that person. Much of who we are is who God created us to be. Choices we make throughout our lives either develop gifts and character, or keep them stilted. We can take pride in using what God has given us, but we cannot become proud, for without him, we are nothing.

We may be tempted to take credit for our socioeconomic status and look down on those with less. While hard work and developing our gifts and talents may have a lot to do with where we stand economically, we must realize that God is the one who has gifted us and has opened opportunities for us to succeed. We shouldn't look down on those who have not done as well. Let God be the judge. "Don't show favoritism. Suppose a man comes into your meeting wearing a gold ring and fine clothes, and a poor man in shabby clothes also comes in. If you show special attention to the man wearing fine clothes and say, 'Here's a good seat for you,' but say to the poor man, 'You stand there' or 'Sit on the floor by my feet' have you not discriminated among yourselves and become judges with evil thoughts?" (James 2:1–4).

When we realize that we are all uniquely gifted, and that we are all uniquely flawed, we are less likely to pass judgment on others. It gives us reason to humbly embrace God's grace for our lives and is motivation to encourage others to accept his grace as well. Only when we see ourselves as God sees us can we see others in the light of truth. "Do not think of yourself more highly than you ought, but think of yourself with sober judgment" (Rom. 12:3). Honest self-examination and asking God to reveal our hearts will enable us to see ourselves as God sees us.

Similarities

While traveling overseas and working with people from twenty-five different countries, I realized how much people are alike. Of course, there are vast cultural differences, but much in our lives is similar. All people have the same basic physical needs: food, shelter, safety, etc. In addition, we have emotional needs: love, approval, concern, and so on. Beyond this, we have spiritual needs: purpose, forgiveness, and relationship with the creator. Typically, the spiritual needs are not as paramount or consistently felt by most people. But at some point, everyone will ask, "Is this all there is, or is there more than just what I can see with my eyes?" There is a deep inner need for God and his grace in our lives. Without God, life is void of deeper meaning; it is random, chaotic, and ultimately pointless.

As Christians we are called to meet the universal physical, emotional, and spiritual needs of others as best we can. Ignoring physical and emotional needs while trying to meet spiritual needs is incomplete. Jesus reached out and met people on every level. He ministered to physical needs when he fed the five thousand, turned the water into wine at a wedding, and healed the blind, lame, and deaf. He ministered to emotional needs when He comforted Mary and Martha when Lazarus died, gave his time and affection to children, and comforted his disciples when he was about to leave them. He ministered to spiritual needs when he forgave sin, freed the demon possessed from their affliction, taught spiritual principles, and provided salvation for the world. He didn't just meet spiritual needs. As we follow Jesus, we should not forget his example and remember to minister to the whole person.

People whose physical and emotional needs have been met are often more open to receive spiritual input. For in meeting the basic needs, we exhibit a spiritual principle of love that reflects the God we serve. We shouldn't meet others needs as a means to an end, but because we genuinely care. To do otherwise is not true love, but manipulation. If someone chooses not to serve God, we need to love them still. God does.

Differences

As well as similarities, dramatic differences exist in culture, personality, motivation, and thinking. Obviously, we were all shaped to some extent by our culture and environment, and are often more "forgiving" or tolerant of these differences. But we are also uniquely different, based on our personalities. I am of the school of thought that considers basic personality as inborn, with individual predispositions that are not learned. These basic personality differences, especially among those we care about deeply, can chafe at us.

The temptation to attribute "right" to people who behave like us and "wrong" to people who are different from us is strong. Even culturally we can fall into that trap. While serving on the missionary ship M.V. Logos, I watched a British gal wash the dishes and set them in the dish rack without rinsing them. My immediate thought was, "That's wrong." I came to realize that it wasn't wrong. It was just a different way of doing dishes. Many times I have been tempted to judge others who are different from me. I immediately want to categorize their way of handling life as "wrong." But often it is, in fact, not wrong, only different.

I am not referring to moral or character issues, or things Scripture outlines as absolutes. We must keep those in view as right or wrong. But in nonabsolutes, we need to be open to change our narcissistic thinking. We need to stop trying to make over mankind in our image.

Many churches have split over issues of preference, rather than issues of morality. Disagreements about worship style have brought division in many churches. Some in the body want to sing worship choruses instead of hymns. Some want to introduce drums and guitars into their morning worship, instead of just the traditional piano and organ. Some want to include drama or dance in the service. Such changes are frequently viewed as "wrong" rather than "different." Style of worship is cultural and based on personal preference and comfort. It is not an absolute. The only absolute about worship is that it should be in spirit and in truth (John 4:23–24). It is a matter of the heart. The outward medium or place is not the issue, though many make it so. Many such preference differences exist within our culture. Those differences are multiplied many times cross culturally. It is sad when the church cannot embrace differences and diversity as a gift.

8

Personality Types

One of the greatest areas of difference is among personality types. Even in their own cultural settings, people just don't "get" each other. While we like to assume others are behaving out of the same set of motivations and perspectives we possess, the truth is that we don't really understand some people at all. Many models for personality type exist. The Myers-Briggs Type Indicator is a basic instrument (assessment) that readily clarifies some of the greatest differences between personalities. While there are many differences within individuals of the same type, there are also prominent similarities. The Myers-Briggs does not indicate pathology (abnormal psych), just basic personality preferences.

When I first heard about personality types as a teenager, I was intrigued, but thought you couldn't so easily summarize a human being or put them in a box. We are fearfully and wonderfully made—all unique like snowflakes. Of course, that is true. People are complex and can't be defined merely by a personality type, but much of their motivation and frame of reference can be understood through awareness of personality types. Isabel Myers, one of the creators of the Myers-Briggs, observed that, "For most people, really understanding their own type in particular, and other people's types in general is a releasing experience, rather than a restricting one." Rather than limiting us, understanding personality types should give us the freedom to explore and develop our natural strengths and recognize our weaknesses. And it should give us the insight to allow others to be who they are without judging them for being different from us. After many years, I have found the study of personality type to be extremely beneficial in accepting people as they are, as God created them. And when their weaknesses rule, I more easily am able to extend grace, not condone sin, but better understand their struggle, which may be different from mine.

In the Myers-Briggs personality profile, four scales with two opposite preferences, for a total of eight areas or functions measure personality type. Each person has a preference on each scale, some stronger than others. Combining the four preferences creates a possibility of sixteen types. While these types will behave in predictable ways much of the time, no one is locked in by their personality. We all exhibit all eight functions, though we usually favor four on a regular basis. The functions are abbreviated by the first letter of the word, except for Intuition, which takes the letter N for an abbreviation, because I is already used for introversion. The four scales are E/I (Extroversion vs. Introversion); S/N (Sensing vs. Intuition); T/F (Thinking vs. Feeling); and J/P (Judging vs. Perceiving).

The following is a brief overview of personality preferences. *Please Understand Me* by David Keirsey and Marilyn Bates and *Please Understand Me II* by David Keirsey provide an in-depth view of the sixteen types if you would like more information.

Extroversion versus Introversion (Focus of Attention and Energy)

Extroversion (E) and Introversion (I) describe a person's preference for either the outer world of people, things, and activities, or the inner world of thoughts and ideas. It is considered one of the earliest preferences to emerge and may be one of the most constant throughout life. The extrovert more often focuses his energy outside of himself, while the introvert prefers to focus his energy internally.

While we all need people in our lives, the extrovert needs more people contact more often, deriving his energy from extroverting. He loves parties and social gatherings where, for him, the hours fly by. If a person is strong on the extrovert scale, he will find it difficult to be alone for any length of time. After a short period of solitude, he will seek out company. The introvert, on the other hand, gains energy from seclusion and quiet activity. Lots of socializing wears him out. For the strong introvert, the minutes at a party seem like hours! Many of us are not extreme extroverts or introverts, but we do all have a preference with which we are more comfortable.

Because extroversion is prominent in our country (75 percent of the population), it is often perceived as the "right" way to be. Those who are introverted are often thought to be unfriendly and unhealthy. I have, in fact, been thought to be stuck up and snobbish when first meeting someone, especially if it is in a group setting. I tend to withdraw and let other people take the lead. But I have been told, after people get to know me that I am not at all like their first impression. I am, they say, actually very warm, friendly, and caring. On occasion, I've been told that I have really changed (for the better), but the reality is that those who said that just didn't know me, so their impression is what has actually changed. In individual settings, it is much more likely that people will peg me as an extrovert. One on one, I am quite comfortable taking the lead and "extroverting." It is common with many introverts to appear extroverted one on one.

Extroverts have a wide network of friends, while introverts tend to have fewer and sometimes deeper relationships. This can cause a lot of relational friction if incorrectly interpreted. Tony, an extreme extrovert frequently talked on two phones at once. He was constantly answering and making calls. It was a little irritating for his introverted wife, Julie. She felt they weren't able to have an uninterrupted conversation or meal together. Tony's ideal evening was to have a bunch of friends over. This is the arena in which he was most comfortable and energized. But Julie was exhausted by having so many people around all the time. It wore her out. She felt inadequate because she wasn't able to meet Tony's companionship needs, and her need for more quiet time with him and time by herself was not being met.

When they began to understand each other's personalities, Tony and Julie were able to compromise and realize the time with friends and alone were both needed to meet their respective preferences. Tony agreed to go to his friends' homes a couple of nights a week, giving Julie quiet time by herself. He also spent quiet evenings at home with his phone turned off, so he could give Julie the uninterrupted time that she needed with him. When they understood that there was a fundamental difference in the way they were wired, they were much happier as a couple and able to meet each other's needs without resentment.

Sensing versus Intuitive (Gathering Information)

The sensing (S) and intuitive (N) dimension refers to ways of perceiving and gathering information. The sensing person may walk into a room and see specific details—the color of the walls, the patterns on upholstery, or the pictures on the wall. They are aware of what is real through their senses. They focus on the concrete and the here and now. The intuitive person walks into a room and the first impression is a global one rather than a specific one. The room is cluttered or bare. It is warm and inviting or cold and functional. The intuitive is aware of meanings and relationships beyond the actual. The intuitive may eventually notice more of the concrete details, but an abstract concept is formed first.

The sensing person is much more grounded in the tangible rather than in the theoretical or possible. They want to deal with the actual and encourage decisions based on facts. Intuitive types enjoy imagination and often look at possibilities and the unknown. While sensing types place great value on history and the present, intuitive types can find themselves always looking to the future, feeling their real life is just around the corner.

The intuitive is much more likely to read between the lines to understand a situation, while the sensing type primarily considers the concrete facts. He would much rather stick with protocol than try something new. The intuitive type will quickly try new or different ways of doing things or solving problems if he feels it is a better way. The sensing type is seen as practical and grounded, while the intuitive type can seem to have his head in the clouds with lots of new ideas. Of the four preferences, this dimension is the source for the most misunderstanding and condemnation of the opposite type.

Charlie, the intuitive artist, is an enigma to his family. At the local university, he majored in art, much to his parents' dismay. Now he occupies his time daydreaming and creating masterpieces. Because he does freelance work, his income is sporadic and undependable. To offset his irregular income, he has chosen to live in modest accommodations and has simplified his lifestyle. The rest of his immediate family is sensing in personality. They don't understand why he would "waste" his life involved in such an unproductive occupation. They badger him about getting a "real" job. Charlie's dad is an auto mechanic and his mom an executive secretary. His brother is an accountant, which makes his parents proud. While Charlie pursues his dream of owning an art gallery, he comes under fire every time he sees his parents. "Why can't you be more like your brother?" or "Did you see the beautiful home your friend George bought? He graduated the same time you did." Charlie's parents view him as flaky and impractical, while he views their lives as boring and mind-numbing.

While these two types of perception and intelligence are quite different, they are both necessary in society. Most artists, musicians, counselors, and novelists are intuitive types. Law enforcers, engineers, surgeons, and office workers are predominantly sensing types. None of us would like a surgeon to operate on us and decide he wanted to try something new and different that day. We appreciate that he will perform the procedure with what has been tried and true, perfecting his talent by doing the same procedure the same way over and over again. In contrast, when a student goes to see his guidance counselor, he doesn't want to hear the same thing the counselor told the last student. She needs to change the direction she steers the student based on his talents and desires by bringing her intuitive talents to the table.

It is interesting to note that most teachers who gravitate toward elementary school are sensing types. They are required to focus on teaching facts. Most classes at that level are fact based and provide the foundation for further learning. By contrast, most teachers who are attracted to teaching college are intuitive types. Typically, college courses require a lot more theory and abstraction than the lower levels. Our world requires both types of intelligence to function effectively.

Thinking versus Feeling (Making Decisions)

The thinking (T) and feeling (F) dimension explores the basis for our decisions. The thinking type base their decisions on the objective, impersonal data and logic, while the feeling type base decisions on how others will be affected and on personal values.

Thinking types value competence in themselves and others, and being respected is a priority. Fulfilling the goal or task is more important than keeping everyone happy. For feeling types, being liked and appreciated is a priority. They value harmony and try to understand other people's points of view and avoid conflict if at all possible. They can become people pleasers if they are not cautious.

The thinking preference is analytical and values fairness and justice. They have the ability to remove themselves from the situation and look at it objectively, focusing on cause and effect in relationship to the goal. The feeling person is sympathetic, and even if not personally involved, will analyze how a decision will impact the people involved. The two types approach problems from opposite angles and will balance each other. They are wise to listen to each other's perspective.

George, a thinking type, was hired as an efficiency consultant for a large company that was struggling financially. The economy had slowed and sales were at an all-time low. George spent weeks familiarizing himself with departments and personnel, looking for solutions to solve the financial crisis. He discovered that the company had been well managed, with departments meeting budget regularly. Spending was not wasteful or extravagant. When sales had started to slow, the company tried various incentives to turn things around and had even dropped product prices. But nothing seemed to make a difference.

George, a thinking type, finally finished his analysis and only had one solution. He told the VP, Phillip, that his recommendation would make an immediate difference in the company's financial standing. He proposed that they make personnel cuts in both sales and production to lower the cost of operation. Phillip, who was a strong feeling type, was devastated. He had known many of these people for ten years, and cared about what happened to them. Phillip didn't want the company to go under, but couldn't bring himself to implement this solution. He asked George to find another option that would exclude layoffs.

George went back to the drawing table and came up with an alternate solution. The company could expand their line and add additional products. It would mean they would have to spend time and money on new production equipment and staff training, but it would help the company to be profitable once again. Even though it would take much longer to see a financial return, it was the solution Phillip decided to implement. His friends and co-workers who had invested years in the company would retain their jobs. It satisfied his need to consider how people would be affected. It also eventually turned the company's finances around. A thinking type VP probably would have employed George's original solution, and many workers would have lost their jobs.

Judging versus Perceiving (Relating to the Outer World)

The judging (J) and perceiving (P) dimension refers to how one interacts with the world around them. Judging types prefer structure and organization, while perceiving types value flexibility and keeping things open-ended. Judging types like to have decisions finalized and appreciate closure, while perceiving types enjoy taking in more information and keeping their options open. These preferences are often reflected in their physical surroundings, with judging types being much neater and more organized than perceiving types, who can tolerate a higher degree of clutter.

The terms judging and perceiving are somewhat misleading. Judging does not refer to being judgmental, but to preferring to have things decided or concluded. And perception does not refer to being perceptive, but to desiring more data before deciding.

Typically judging types avoid change, while perceiving types more often enjoy change. If not careful, judging types can become inflexible and dogmatic, while perceiving types can procrastinate so much that they fall far short of their potential. Work demands may require a person to behave in their less-preferred functions. Having to be on schedule and operate within a strong structure may cause perceiving types to behave like judging types at work, but that doesn't change their true preference.

Jonathan and Gary grew up best friends since middle school. They went their separate ways in college, and both were involved in busy careers, so they saw each other infrequently. While both were still single, they decided to take a two-week beach vacation together. Jonathan, a judging type, suggested three possible places he'd like to visit, and Gary, a perceiving type, said he would do some research on them. Gary compiled extensive information on cost, weather, housing options, and local activities for each city and also for a few other places that he'd thought about visiting. Jonathan was a little overwhelmed with all of the information Gary presented to him, but made his choice, hoping their destination would be settled. Gary wanted to do a little more research and didn't want to lock in quite yet. Over the next few weeks, Jonathan became anxious for the decision to be made. He pushed Gary to make a final decision, frustrated that his friend was so indecisive. Gary resisted making a decision, searching endlessly online for the perfect accommodations that would be ocean-front, reasonably priced, with the best view, and closest to fun attractions. Finally, when he had to make a decision or pay several hundred dollars more for airline tickets, he finalized their accommodations, and they purchased their tickets.

Jonathan wasn't comfortable until the decision was finalized, but Gary needed the extra time to research and make sure they knew everything about each area. He wasn't able to make a final decision until he thoroughly examined all options. Often a deadline pushes a perceiving type to wind it up. Fortunately, the rising cost of tickets forced Gary to closure before Jonathan had a nervous breakdown.

My Personality Type

Much like being left-handed, I also prefer introversion, intuition, feeling and perceiving. Of course, I don't use my left hand exclusively. Nor do I use my preferred personality traits exclusively. But it is more natural for me to exhibit the INFP functions. Because 75 percent of both genders in America are extroverted and sensing, my introverted, intuitive functions are somewhat out of step with the majority. In the feeling dimension, I am in line with most female Americans. It is the only dimension that has a different statistic for male and female, with 65 percent of females prefer the feeling and 60 percent of males prefer the thinking preference. The judging and perceiving functions are divided equally among Americans, with 50 percent preferring each. Knowing that I am a minority personality type—only 1 percent of the American population is INFP—gives me the freedom to be who I was created to be and not feel the pressure to conform to the majority. Though INFP's are a small minority in the general population, I found it interesting that ten of eleven students in a graduate seminar class for English teachers were INFP. Counselors are also largely NF types. Our personalities have a strong influence on our interests and vocation.

The Myers-Briggs emphasizes that every type has positive aspects and strengths. Weaknesses are also examined, but not in a fatalistic way. Growth and development of lesser preferences is encouraged. Many basic personality differences are not understood by those of other temperaments; thus the dissimilarities can produce great misunderstanding and friction in relationships. When the personality model is understood, much of the frustration caused by differences disappears.

9

Motivating Forces

Temperament and Motivation

Depending on the particular combination of traits, the Myers-Briggs defines four basic personality types within the sixteen models. If one doesn't understand the basic motivating force in each type, it is easy to project our motives onto others and critique them accordingly, often grossly erring in our understanding of a person's behavior. Typically, we assign negative rather than positive motives to differing behavior.

Power (12 percent of population)

The NT (intuitive-thinking) temperament is motivated by his intelligence and the power that intelligence provides. He wants to be able to understand, control, predict, and explain whatever his particular field requires. He gravitates towards the fields of science and technology, where he enjoys the complexity and abstraction of ideas. His need for competence and power is the driving force behind his actions; this is carried across into his leisure, as well as his work.

Spirit (12 percent of population)

The NF (intuitive-feeling) temperament is more concerned with becoming or self-actualization of himself and others. Being authentic and real are extremely important for the NF. While NF's search for meaning and integrity above all else, they want others to understand their unique contributions to the world. Their focus is on relationships and interaction, wanting to help others reach their full potential.

Duty (38 percent of population)

The SJ's (sensing-judging) goal is to be useful to society and their particular social unit or position. They feel it is their obligation to give, serve, and care for those around them. SJ's gladly take on responsibility and are thrilled when they are recognized for who they are—the backbone of society. They are the most traditional of the temperaments; they value rules, conformity, order, and unchanging structure.

Action (38 percent of population)

The SP's (sensing-perceiving) goal is to live freely and spontaneously. SP's live for the enjoyment of whatever they are doing today. They are not focused on duty or tomorrow, but only fulfilling their immediate impulses. The SP views action as its own end rather than a means to an end, as most of the other temperaments view action. More than those with any other temperament, excitement and adventure drives him.

Don't Assign Motives

While these driving motives are simplified here, they do characterize the types in general. Our driving force can and often will be totally different from another person's. We should also keep in mind that culture, upbringing, and religious beliefs will influence our natural inclinations and drives. As people grow and develop, they often exhibit a variety of personality traits, though their true type remains their most comfortable and natural realm.

Because God is the only one who is able to completely understand a person's motives and intentions, we are wise to refrain from assigning motives to other's actions. Of course, if we see patterns in behavior, we will naturally surmise motives, but we must be careful not to become dogmatic within our hearts or to accuse another directly of negative intentions. To abstain from projecting and assuming motives goes against our natural inclination, but doing so will allow us to be much more accepting of people who are different from us.

God's Word Exalts Differences

Comparing ourselves to others is futile, as is using ourselves to evaluate others. We should use Jesus and his word to assess ourselves. As we acknowledge God's incredible plan to use many different kinds of people and personalities to accomplish his will, we are humbled. If we allow him to, he can and will use us in our uniqueness for his glory.

First Corinthians 12 discusses differing gifts, differing body parts, and differing functions of the church. It is a chapter that exalts diversity as necessary and as God's will. We should not and cannot all be alike. If all received the gift of administration, the church would be lopsided. Administrators must administrate. If everyone administrated, there would be no one to administrate over. And we can't all be preachers. Preachers need a congregation to whom they preach. We can't all stand in the pulpit! When viewed in this context, it seems obvious that we shouldn't and can't all operate from the same vantage point or framework. As well as having many similarities, we are wonderfully fundamentally different in many ways. We should all try to understand others' perspectives, allowing them the leeway to express their gifts in their own way.

"But in fact God has arranged the parts in the body, every one of them, just as he wanted them to be. If they were all one part, where would the body be? As it is, there are many parts, but one body" (1 Cor. 12:18–20). It is part of God's creative genius that we are not all alike. Over the years, I have been in many church services that have used candles for an object lesson. The point is often that one person's light can be shared with another, and as each person passes it on, the light eradicates the darkness. The visual is quite impressive, especially if the room is initially completely dark. I recently attended such a service. Instead of an actual candle flame being passed on, glow sticks were handed out and at the same time everyone "lit" their glow stick by snapping it. All different color glow sticks were represented around the room. It struck me as a great illustration of not just our illuminating, but our illuminating with our individual gifts and talents to make a beautiful collage of color. Each of us is a different soul color, and each has unique gifts and talents to offer the world. How sad if we expect everyone else to be the same soul color that we are.

No Excuse for Weaknesses

While each personality type has natural strengths and weaknesses, we should not feel our fate is predetermined because of our personality type. All types can develop both their primary and inferior preferences, growing into stronger, more-talented individuals. And knowing your personality type does not automatically excuse your weaknesses. It may explain them, but it doesn't give you a pass. We are all going to be held accountable for our lives one day. I can't tell God I am an INFP, so he needs to excuse me for sin that I am naturally inclined toward. Of course, he is already intimately aware of how he made me, and he expects me to strengthen the gifts and talents he has instilled and work on ridding myself of the weaknesses. He has promised to help in this process, if I am willing to submit myself to him. Not only does such obedient submission glorify him, it saves me from much darkness.

Corey had a dynamic take-charge personality; he was an ENTJ personality type. After finding that an employee he'd hired hadn't followed protocol on a project, he let her have it, verbally cutting her to shreds. Later, when talking about how guilty he felt for belittling this woman, he stated, "I don't know why she made me do it," blaming the employee's failure to follow protocol for his bad behavior. Not only was it the employee's fault, it was also God's fault. "That's just the way God made me," he stated defensively.

While the circumstances revealed an area of weakness or temptation for Corey, the woman didn't make him behave in an abrasive, verbally abusive fashion. He chose to do that. By blaming God for making him that way, he was letting himself off of the hook, thus justifying his behavior and dismissing the need for true repentance or requirement for change.

Corey felt guilty for his bad behavior, but didn't take his sorrow to God, accept responsibility for his actions, and ask for forgiveness. His was not true repentance. For in the same breath that he said he felt bad, he justified his actions and blamed the other party and God. "Godly sorrow brings repentance that leads to salvation and leaves no regret, but worldly sorrow brings death" (2 Cor. 7:10).

When we understand our personality weaknesses, we can guard ourselves and take extra precautions against giving in to our weaknesses, rather than excusing them. Yes, we all have tendencies to sin, some in one area, and some in another. We must be aware of the "sin that so easily entangles" us (Heb. 12:1) and guard against it, taking the "way out" (1 Cor. 10:13) God promises to provide for us.

SECTION III: PERSONALITY REALITIES

OVERVIEW

Summary

We must avoid measuring others by ourselves. God has created all of us uniquely; therefore, we are no better or worse than any other person. Differences in personality types can help us understand each other on a much deeper level, bringing more peace into relationships. God loves and has created diversity among his children. We need our differences to build each other up and for balance to accomplish God's purposes. Knowing our personality weaknesses does not give us an excuse for them; it gives insight for positive change.

Light Reality

• We should understand differences as just that, not as rights and wrongs.

• Since differences are most exacerbated in close personal relationships where expectations are greatest, we must choose to embrace and appreciate differences in our family, friends, and coworkers.

• Recognizing our personality type will free us to pursue our unique strengths and be aware of and shore up our natural weaknesses.

• Acknowledging basic differences in motivation will create respect and appreciation for others.

Dark Reality

• When we measure others by ourselves, we become rigid and arrogant, unable to flexibly work with others.

- When we view differences as wrong, we will be frustrated and impatient with others because they never meet our distorted expectations.
- When we don't appreciate how God made us each different, our minds will focus on the negative in others, rather than others' unique positive contributions.

Reality Discussion Questions

1. What has shaped your view of right and wrong?

_____

_____

2. Are there spiritual areas where you judge others as wrong who are really only different? Explain.

_____

_____

3. How do our differences compliment and encourage our spiritual growth?

_____

_____

4. When you work or live with someone with a different personality, do you respect their differences or find them irritating? Give an example:

_____

_____

5. Of the four personality motivators, what is your primary motivation? Power, spirit, duty, or action?

_____

_____

6. What is your gut reaction to those who have a different motivating force?

_____

_____

7. What weaknesses have you excused as "just the way you are"?

_____

_____

8. How will you work on these weaknesses, rather than excuse them?

_____

_____

9. Retake the quiz at the beginning of Personality Realities. Did you change any of your answers? Which ones and why?

_____

_____

Prayer

Heavenly Father, thank you for the great diversity among your children. Give me wisdom to understand the distinction between absolutes and those things that are merely preferences or personalities. Please help me to appreciate and embrace differences, rather than judge them as wrong. Forgive me for judging. Allow me to use my unique strengths for your glory. Allow me to recognize my weaknesses and strengthen them with your help. In Jesus' name, amen.

SECTION IV: REAL AUTHORITY

Quiz

Multiple Choice Stories

Choose the *best* answer to the questions below.

1. Ashley works as an administrative assistant for a large law firm. She is well respected for her efficient and personable handling of clients and staff. More importantly, she is a person of extraordinary integrity. Ashley works closely with the paralegals helping them with copies, faxes, e-mails, and word processing. She also verifies their hours. Last week Daniel, a paralegal, left several times without signing out and then handed in an inflated tally. Ashley noticed the discrepancy and confronted him. He told her it was none of her business; she should submit his falsified hours. He explained that he had important errands to run during business hours. He reasoned that the attorneys padded their expenses, so why shouldn't he? Ashley explained that she felt it would be dishonest for her to submit the additional hours. The attorneys trust her to verify paralegal hours; the attorney's hours are their own responsibility. Daniel insisted that she follow his instructions, reminding her that she is just a lowly assistant. Ashley knows that submitting the falsified hours would be wrong, but she is concerned Daniel will try to get her fired if she reports his actual work hours.

What should she do?

   a. She should do as Daniel requested; his position is higher than hers. She is not lying about her hours, so it doesn't make a difference. She needs her job.

b. She should inform her supervising attorney about Daniel's inflated hours. Her job is to verify hours. She should report the correct hours.

c. She should submit the correct amount of hours without saying anything to anyone.

d. She should quit. She is under too much pressure.

2. Eric graduated from the University of Connecticut two years ago and opened a successful Italian restaurant in the heart of Manhattan. In his personal life, his parents and his newlywed wife are loving and supportive. In the business arena, he has a large network of friends and acquaintances mentoring him. Over the last two years Eric has bought a new Mercedes, a Harley, a home in the suburbs, a vacation home in the mountains, and a condo on the ocean. He is living his dream, but something seems to be missing. He has a fantastic family, brilliant mentors, and has been able to afford everything he ever wanted, so why isn't he satisfied? He asks for advice from friends and family and gets a variety of suggestions.

Which is the best advice?

a. His cousin Justin tells him to visualize himself happy and fulfilled, and it will happen. He needs to believe it, and that will bring it about.

b. His best friend, Jonathan, tells him about eastern religions and meditation. He advises Eric to focus on his oneness with the universe; that will bring him peace.

c. His mom, a Christian, tells him he will only find peace in a relationship with God. What he is missing is a relationship with his creator.

d. His wife, Danielle, tells him he just needs a vacation. He's been working too hard and needs to get away for a week or two. She suggests a Caribbean cruise.

TRUE OR FALSE?

Real Authority

True/False 1. We should each be the ultimate authority for what is right and wrong for us.

True/False 2. All religions should have equal authority in our lives.

True/False 3. Following the authority of God's word is primarily following a list of do's and don'ts.

True/False 4. If you don't agree with a policy at work, you don't have to follow it unless the boss is around.

True/False 5. God's laws exist primarily for our benefit.

True/False 6. Listening to a sermon each week is the best way to know God's word.

True/False 7. It is okay to break the law as long as no one gets hurt.

True/False 8. It is easiest to learn tough lessons through our own mistakes.

True/False 9. Appropriate parental authority allows the child to do whatever he wants.

True/False 10. When I don't submit to authority, I am only hurting myself.

10

Follow the Owner's Manual

"Jesus said, 'If you hold to my teaching, you are really
my disciples. Then you will know the truth, and the truth
will set you free.'" (John 8:31–32)

Why Use the Manual?

Have you ever tried to put something together without looking at the directions or owner's manual? I have—more times than I'd like to admit. After I've made a mess of things, I finally, out of desperation, consult the manual. At that point, I wonder why I didn't take the obvious shortcut and start there.

American society, of which I am a product, is extremely individualistic compared to many in the world. We don't like to depend on anyone but ourselves. We can make our own way, figure it out all by ourselves, and are proud to be self-made. While independence is necessary to be a successful adult, we would help ourselves by consulting the owner's manual. After all, we didn't create ourselves, so how do we know what is best for us?

In Rick Warren's *Purpose Driven Life,* he opens with this statement: "It is not about you." While it is impossible to remove ourselves totally from subjective perspectives on life, we can begin to see more objectively by submitting to an outside measure of reality. Pastor Warren builds a wonderful understanding that we are in God's world, not the reverse. God is the center. We are a subject in his world. But sadly many of us try to make God a subject in our world.

We place ourselves at the center of the universe and expect, if not demand, to be the priority. In doing so, we are acting out of alignment with the real order of the universe; consequently, we are making life more difficult for ourselves. We end up straying from the light reality into darkness and paying unnecessary soul toll.

When we determine our steps based on our subjective theories and experience, rather than on His objective word and intervention in our lives, we often miss the mark. Of course, if we are Christian and have a relationship with God, our relationship is to some extent subjective. God speaks to us, comforts and guides us, but the relationship must be measured in submission to His objective word. Anything less, and we position ourselves as the measure for truth—a very dangerous place indeed.

A deep discussion on Christian apologetics is not necessary at this point, but it is an important issue to settle if one is going to accept the Bible as our Owner's Manual. For those unfamiliar with the term Christian apologetics, it is the defense of the divine origin and authority of Christianity. I have often thought about Josh McDowell's discussion: Who is Jesus Christ? Lord, liar, or lunatic. He proposes that many people's opinion that Jesus was a great moral teacher, but not God, is not an option. Jesus claimed to be God. If that claim was true, then he is Lord, and we can either accept or reject him as our Lord. If that claim was false, then he either deliberately lied making him a liar, or he was deluded, and thus a lunatic. If he was a liar or a lunatic, he does not qualify as a great teacher. Based on the facts, that option doesn't exist. He is one of the three: Lord, liar, or lunatic. We must each decide what we believe.

Many decades ago, I settled the truth of God's word and Christianity in my mind, heart, and soul. But if this is an issue for you, then Josh McDowell's *Evidence that Demands a Verdict* and Hal Seed and Dan Grider's *The God Questions* are both excellent resources.

Following the Manual Keeps Us on Track

Jesus expected his disciples to follow his teaching because of who he was. He was God (John 14:10), Savior (Luke 2:11), and Lord (John 13:13) and proved it through his life, his words, and his miracles. No human has ever come close to living the life that Jesus lived. His love, wisdom, and power are unparalleled. According to Jesus, those who acknowledge the truth about him and who desire to be his disciples must respond to his commands with submission. And he promised that submission to his commands brings a greater understanding of truth. Furthermore, a greater understanding of truth brings greater freedom. Spiritual freedom brings greater joy, peace, and happiness—all of the things for which individuals deeply long. "Jesus said, 'If you hold to my teaching, you are really my disciples. Then you will know the truth, and the truth will set you free'" (John 8:31–32).

Obviously, no one always submits to His commands. "We all stumble in many ways" (James 3:2), and beyond stumbling, we sin. "If we claim to be without sin, we deceive ourselves and the truth is not in us" (1 John 1:8). Life is a struggle; it is challenging to live as God intended. But the more we submit to His commands and follow His ways, rather than our own, the more we know the truth and are set free. When we choose to follow Jesus, we begin a lifelong process, with no shortcuts or quick fixes. We live one day at a time—failing, falling, and getting back up. Other times we succeed in following and obeying. When we do fall, we ask for forgiveness, gratefully accept it, make right any injured relationships, and move forward.

When I was a teenager I heard an analogy that I still remember today. God's word and commands are like the tracks for a train. We are the train. When following the tracks, we can proceed forward with the least resistance and trouble. But when the train goes off the tracks, it crashes. It was not made for the road or meadow, but for the train tracks. It is most free when following the tracks for which it was created. When the train attempts to move forward without the tracks, it ends in destruction and disappointment. When we take our lives off the tracks of God's commands, we wander from the light path into darkness.

What are God's Commands?

Jesus said his commands are not burdensome, but light (Matt. 11:30). All of his commands are built on one foundation and can be summarized in one word: LOVE. "Love the Lord your God with all your heart and with all your soul and with all your strength and with all your mind, and love your neighbor as yourself" (Luke 10:27). We are to love God and to love our neighbor as ourselves. Love is not burdensome.

While the Old Testament listed many detailed rules and rituals, the New Testament tells us they were set in place to reveal our sinfulness (Rom. 3:20). They were established to show us that we can never measure up, because we can never keep all the commands. They lead us to faith in Christ, who did measure up and who has offered us forgiveness. Jesus' death was the price for our sins, not his own. He now offers to stand between us and God, as our mediator. We don't deserve His forgiveness or mercy, but it is there for the taking because of His great love for us.

But what is love? In order to fully understand true love, we need to understand who Jesus is. He was, is, and always will be God. Jesus existed before he was born on earth. He lived in heaven, a perfect place where God his father exits. Scripture tells us he willingly came to earth. "Who being very nature God, did not consider equality with God something to be grasped, but made himself nothing, taking the very nature of a servant, being made in human likeness. And being found in appearance as a man, he humbled himself and became obedient to death—even death on a cross!" (Phil. 2:6–8). What a picture of sacrificial love. God becomes man to save man. "God made him who had no sin to be sin for us, so that in him we might become the righteousness of God" (2 Cor. 5:21). He was pure and holy, but he became sin for us, so that we could have God's favor and eternal life. That is love.

Study and Submit to the Owner's Manual

In order to fully understand God's love, we should study, meditate on and submit to His word daily. It is our guide and our only true owner's manual. We should want to follow him, out of gratitude for what he has done. But if not gratitude, let your selfishness guide you! Do it for yourself. God's word will bring only benefit and good into your life. If you don't have noble motives for following God's word, this pragmatic motive can bring you to his word, which can transform a selfish heart into a selfless, grateful heart.

When we live by our own standards, we are never sure if we are actually choosing what is best. We are guessing and hoping we are making good choices. When we are sure of God's principles, we can know we are fulfilling his purposes. Our meaning, direction, and life goals are revealed. Our priorities are clarified. Of course, outside of clear biblical direction, we all need to make directional decisions (where to live, what job to accept, etc.), but the deeper character and soul issues are already decided. We don't need to spend time debating or evaluating those black-and-white issues, such as honesty, integrity, and morality. They are laid out clearly in Scripture.

In order to know what the creator has planned, and how we will function best in his world, we must study his manual. It is there for us to digest and assimilate into our lives. Scripture is our spiritual food, necessary for our spiritual growth and understanding. We cannot follow the manual if we don't know what it contains. None of us considers going very long without food, but how many of us who claim to be following God are on a spiritual starvation diet. We eat sparingly, if at all, from the feast he has prepared for us. Just as healthy food brings strength to the weak, partaking of Scripture's truth can bring renewal and transformation to our souls.

And when we delve into the depths of his spiritual treasures, what do we do with them? To refuse to submit to what he has instructed in his manual is prideful. It is saying, "God doesn't know best. I am the God of my universe." Setting oneself up as God is dangerous. He is the one who gives you life and sustains you every day. The prince of this world decided he wanted to be on God's level, and his future is set. And it's not pretty. "And the devil, who deceived them, was thrown into the lake of burning sulfur. . . . They will be tormented day and night for ever and ever" (Rev. 20:10). Some like to view hell as a big party, but they are mistaken. It is not a place to go for fun and pleasure. Hell has no presence of God who is love, light, and all things good. Hell is not where you want to spend eternity.

"Do not merely listen to the word, and so deceive yourselves. Do what it says. Anyone who listens to the word but does not do what it says is like a man who looks at his face in a mirror and, after looking at himself, goes away and immediately forgets what he looks like. But the man who looks intently into the perfect law that gives freedom, and continues to do this, not forgetting what he has heard, but doing it—he will be blessed in what he does" (James 1:22–25). How must we look at God's word? Intently. It is not a casual, haphazard or occasional looking, but one with intention. *Webster's Collegiate Dictionary* defines *intently* as "directed with strained or eager attention: concentrated." Such looking promises to bring freedom and blessing.

See Appendix II for more great reasons to make the Bible your well used owner's manual.

11

Choices and Consequences

Rules, Rules, Rules

It is natural to question authority and ask why we should behave in a certain way. Often, those who are most intelligent question and rebel the most. Rules should make sense; policies and laws shouldn't be arbitrary or in place just for the sake of control. But because earthly rule-makers are human, there will be no perfect set of earthly rules, nor will we find a perfect government. And unless those in authority are telling us to blatantly violate God's law, we should submit. "Therefore, it is necessary to submit to the authorities, not only because of possible punishment but also because of conscience" (Rom. 13:5).

But God's laws are beyond human. They were crafted with our benefit in mind. Submission to these rules is similar to a child submitting to the rules of a wise parent. The parent has the child's best interest at heart. When the child submits, life goes well because the child doesn't bring heartache on himself or herself. But when children break the rules, they often bring trouble into their own lives. In most cases, the parents' rules weren't set out of a desire for power or control, but for protection and love. "Don't touch the hot stove." "Stay out of the street." "Wash your hands before you eat." These rules are for the child's benefit, not the parent's. If the child ignores the admonitions he could get burned, hit by a car, or get sick. Following the commands protects the child.

God promises to discipline those he loves. "My son, do not despise the Lord's discipline and do not resent his rebuke, because the Lord disciplines those he loves, as a father the son he delights in" (Prov. 3:11–12). He understands that it is unpleasant to be disciplined, but it is for our good, for when we respond correctly discipline is a catalyst for growth. "No discipline seems pleasant at the time, but painful. Later on, however, it produces a harvest of righteousness and peace for those who have been trained by it" (Heb. 12:11). God our great Father knows that we need discipline and consequences to create strong character.

If you are a parent, you would do well to follow his example; don't hesitate to discipline your children, for you are molding their character and keeping them from committing the same offenses over and over and developing bad soul habits that result in leaving the safe, light path. "Tough love" as Dr. James Dobson calls it, is true love. Letting a child get away with anything is not love. "The rod of correction imparts wisdom, but a child left to himself disgraces his mother" (Prov. 29:15). Proverbs 13:24 goes so far as saying those who don't discipline their children, hate them.

God is a good, loving parent. His rules are in place for our good and protection. And His discipline is for our growth and development. God is not controlling and vindictive, as many people believe. While there may be earthly parents who correct with impure motives, we can know that our loving creator always has our best interest in mind.

Facing the Consequences

When we break the rules, we often bring punishment and negative consequences on ourselves. Why do we knowingly create more trouble when "each day has enough trouble of its own" (Matt. 6:34)? When you speed, you get a ticket, and some of your hard-earned money goes toward "stupid tax." Dave Ramsey coined this phrase in reference to monetary loss due to bad decisions we make.

But worse than "stupid tax" that costs you money is soul toll that damages your soul. Romans 13:5 refers to submitting, not just because of possible punishment, but because of conscience. The soul toll for not submitting is immense. When we don't submit to authority, we are placing ourselves above the authority and above our conscience. We are exhibiting pride, rebellion, and deception—self-deception. In essence we are saying, "I should be above this authority. I am entitled to break this rule/law, etc." Pride is at the root of all kinds of evil; avoid it at all cost. When we are proud, we damage our soul and become blind to the truth. "God opposes the proud but gives grace to the humble" (James 4:6). I don't know about you, but I'd prefer that God not oppose me.

Our God-given conscience knows it is right to submit to authority, so when we do not, we are damaging our conscience. Scripture clearly explains that when we repeatedly ignore or act contrary to our conscience, we in effect disable it and render it useless, making it a "seared conscience" (1 Tim. 4:2). We set ourselves up for justifying and rationalizing our action or inaction. "Today, if you hear his voice, do not harden your hearts" (Heb. 4:7b). If we continue on this course long enough, we will eventually believe our own lie and become self-deceived. If we continue on the path of self-deception, our growth will be stunted and God's ability to work in and through our lives will be greatly hindered.

When we choose to go our own way and ignore the authority over our lives, it is to our own detriment. Depending on the offense, there could be job loss, broken relationships or, if serious enough, incarceration, as well as emotional pain and suffering and spiritual decline.

Submit, Despite Disagreeing

"He who rebels against the authority is rebelling against what God has instituted, and those who do so will bring judgment on themselves. For rulers hold no terror for those who do right, but for those who do wrong." (Rom. 13:2–3)

One out of every 100 adult Americans was behind bars at the beginning of 2008, making America the number-one incarcerator in the world (*USA Today*, March 2, 2008). Why is our prison population the largest per capita in the world? Are our laws unreasonably strict? I don't believe that is the case. Many countries have laws that are far more rigid and harsh than America—look at laws in any Muslim country. People can be imprisoned for speaking freely, women are punished for appearing in public without their veils, and one woman was even incarcerated for naming a teddy bear Mohammed. A British teacher in Sudan, Gillian Gibbons, faced up to forty lashes, a fine, and imprisonment when she allowed her seven-year-old students to name their class teddy bear Mohammed. The bear was named after a popular student in the class, but a school secretary reported she had named it after the prophet Mohammed. The original charge was blasphemy. Fortunately, British politicians became involved and the sentence was reduced to inciting religious hatred, and she was sentenced to fifteen days in prison. Certainly, by comparison, we do not have overly harsh or strict policies in America that cause our prisons to be full.

America is a nation that has lost respect for authority. As individuals, we want to make our own rules and laws and live by our own standards. So we do. And sometimes we pay the consequences by being locked up. But even if we don't get caught, we always pay the consequences for rebelling. Pride and arrogance grow, creating a hard heart that repels rather than attracts truth.

No government will execute perfect laws, because every government is human. But, even if we don't agree, it is our obligation to follow the rules of the government and other institutions that have authority over us at any given time. While it is easier to comply when we understand, we may not always understand or agree with policies. But Scripture clearly instructs us to submit to authority (unless the law clearly violates God's Word).

Many times, laws and policies we don't agree with or understand are neutral. They are seemingly arbitrary procedures that neither benefit nor hurt us directly, like speed limits. They are in place to keep traffic safe and orderly. They could be five miles higher or lower and still provide the desired outcome.

Often, people obey the laws of the government for fear of reprisal, such as a traffic ticket, but are not as concerned when it comes to other authorities in their lives. For example, Dan's office has a policy of no overtime without approval. He occasionally needs to stay to finish a project, so he calls his supervisor, Tim, and gets the necessary permission. Tim is usually a little hesitant and asks Dan several questions about the need for additional time, but has never declined his request. Dan knows that the rule is in place to keep people from costing the company unnecessary overtime, but he knows he is a good worker who doesn't abuse the system, and feels they should make an exception for him. He believes he shouldn't have to get permission.

So one day Dan decides to ignore policy and stays late without permission. He figures Tim never sees the timecards and will not be the wiser. But what he doesn't realize is that when Dan calls to request overtime, Tim always sends an e-mail to the payroll department, letting them know he approved Dan's additional hours. When Dan's card shows up with overtime and no e-mail from Tim, payroll calls Tim to ask about it. Of course, he hadn't approved it, so he calls Dan into his office. Dan mumbles something about having forgotten to get permission and avoids eye contact with Tim. Tim suspects he is lying.

This seemingly minor offense has several consequences. Dan is given a written warning, which is also placed in his personnel file. Tim feels that

Dan was being dishonest about forgetting to get permission. He decides that he can't trust Dan to be honest with him, so he doesn't want him in a management position in the company. The promotion Tim had planned give to Dan is given to someone else. And this offense has also hurt their working relationship. Tim will now wonder when Dan is telling the truth and when he is lying. Trust will have to be rebuilt. Also, if Dan is written up two more times for any offense, he likely will lose his job. The company is strict with their three strikes-and-you're-out policy.

The above includes the outward results of Dan's action. But what about the spiritual consequences? Dan has violated his conscience by refusing to submit to the authority over him. He knows he should have requested permission, but he didn't. Dan's pride overruled his honesty; he convinced himself he was above the rules. The rules, he rationalized, were for other people. When a person continues on this path of lying to himself and acting as if he is above the rules, he may eventually deceive himself. Initially he justified and manipulated the facts, but eventually he begins to believe a lie. The further he gets from the truth, the more distorted his thinking and life become. Persistent resistance of the truth, also known as habitual sin, can result in a life that is out of touch with reality.

The good news is that Dan was caught, and being caught likely will short-circuit any new habit he may have otherwise developed. And the discipline he received probably will be a deterrent to future offenses. But unless he truly repents (confesses his sin to God and turns away from it), and is not just sorry that he got caught, he may only outwardly submit, but continue with an attitude of pride, which will whittle away at his good character. Dan needs to be humbled by his actions. God's goodness in allowing him to be caught offered an opportunity to change his ways before his ways change him.

Often, the excuse for ignoring authority is that everyone else is ignoring authority. It is a trap to think that something is acceptable because everyone else is doing it. Majority acceptance doesn't automatically make something right, even if society promotes that relativism. We cannot measure ourselves by ourselves. God and his word are the true measure for acceptable and good living. Submitting to his authority brings the peace and happiness for which everyone longs.

12

Secondhand Student

Take a Short Cut

Many people have learned the hard way by breaking Scriptural principles. They have paid the soul toll, so it is helpful if we listen to their story, for it will save us similar soul toll. But few of us seem to take this shortcut. We want to make our own mistakes, so we end up learning the hard way. While there is great benefit from being independent and making our own decisions, there is also incredible benefit from learning from others' mistakes. To be so independent that we won't listen to those who have had pertinent life experience is to be self-destructive.

One example is cosigning for another person's financial obligation. Scripture warns against this. "He who puts up security for another will surely suffer, but whoever refuses to strike hands in pledge is safe" (Prov. 11:15, see also Prov. 6:1–5).

When Carla's daughter Nichole was ready to move into an apartment with her friends, she asked her mother to cosign for her because she hadn't yet established any credit. Nichole had a good job at a doctor's office and was diligent about paying her bills on time. But there were three other women on the lease, two of whom didn't have jobs. Carla's friend Clair told her she thought it was a bad idea, because two of the women were not working. Clair had cosigned for her son, John, and ended up bailing him out when one of his roommates filed bankruptcy, and the other was M.I.A. No one could locate him. The apartment complex from which they had rented, wanted a settlement for a broken lease and two month's rent that the other two boys hadn't paid. Because Clair had cosigned for her son, she was about to be sued if she didn't pay their request. With no other choice, she paid the settlement. She didn't want to see her friend Carla trapped in a similar situation.

John, Clair's son, was Nichole's friend. Not wanting her to get into the bad situation he had gone through, he urged her not to sign a lease with two unemployed friends. Nichole was sure they would find work soon, and it wouldn't be an issue. She was engaging in wishful or magical thinking, believing everything would be fine because that is what she wanted. It is an easy trap to fall into. Be on guard against magical thinking.

Against Clair's advice, Carla co-signed for Nichole. And against John's advice, Nichole signed the lease with her three friends. Three months later they both wished they had listened to their respective friends. Nichole's two unemployed friends still had no jobs, and Carla, Nichole's mom, had paid their portion of the rent so her daughter's credit wouldn't be ruined. While she was trying to protect Nichole, she had become an enabler to the two lazy roommates. Carla didn't know what to do to break the cycle. She wished she had listened to Clair's advice.

Nichole felt bad about her mother covering the rent shortfall, so she started pressuring the two unemployed roommates to find work. The four roommates' relationships became strained. The other working friend was also fed up with the unemployed roommates hanging around, messing up the apartment all week, never doing dishes or cleaning up after themselves. She joined Nichole in confronting their irresponsibility. The nonworking roommates concocted excuses and lies about why they weren't working or helping around the apartment. What started as a friendly, fun atmosphere in the apartment turned into a "them against us" dance.

God puts us in relationships so that others can be there for us, and we can be there for those around us. We should not consider honest advice and wisdom from those who have been in similar situations as meddlesome. If advice is given with the right attitude, as was the case in the above situation, we should seriously consider what is being said. God is giving us a shortcut! We don't have to learn the hard way. We can learn the easy way—from someone else's mistakes.

Be grateful, and take a few shortcuts in life! It is much less painful.

A World without Ultimate Authority

God's word says he has written his laws on our hearts (Heb. 8:10). Our consciences bear witness to what is right and wrong. Because our upbringing and culture affect our God-given conscience, we cannot blindly trust our conscience. Unfortunately, American society has slowly drifted from God's standards in many areas. Many unwise things have become the norm and acceptable. Often the standard is that you can do whatever you want, "as long as it's not hurting anybody else." But often poor choices cost the one making them. And a person who is paying soul toll has less to offer those around them, so the ripple will affect many negatively. Poor choices are in fact hurting others, even if it is not readily apparent.

Imagine a world where there is no ultimate truth or reality. Everyone decides for himself what is right—what he feels like doing—and acts accordingly. If murder seems right, then it is right. If lying and cheating is the expedient thing to do, then it is done. If adultery seems the most appealing option, then it is carried out. Moral chaos and decline would rule the day. There would be wars, and suicide bombers would murder innocent civilians, believing it was the right thing to do. Selfishness, disrespect, and cruelty would be rampant. People would create viruses to infiltrate other people's computers, just because they could. Thieves would steal because it was more appealing than work. The prisons would be full, with the authorities having to release inmates early to make room for all those living by their own truth and submitting to their own authority. I guess it is not too hard to imagine, because that is our world.

Any honest person will admit that much of life is hard. To be human is to know pain and suffering. Trials and struggles vary from person to person, but all are included in experiencing the results of the Fall. No one is exempt. So why do we make choices that create more hardship? It is time we minimize the damage and make choices that align with the ultimate authority. Doing so brings less heartache and more freedom and blessing. God's way is always better than our way. Initially, loving God and our fellow-human may seem harder and take more courage, but, in the long run, following the principles of love that He has ordained leads to our best, most fulfilling life. A life following the owner's manual is a life that glorifies God.

SECTION IV: REAL AUTHORITY
OVERVIEW

Summary

God's word lays out a plan for every person's life. When we accept that his intentions toward us are good and better than anything we could plan for ourselves, we understand the importance of consulting the owner's manual. When we submit to his word and the authorities over us, our lives will reap the rewards he has promised, and we will glorify him.

Light Reality

- Learn what the word of God has to say. Study it, meditate on it and digest it.
- Follow what the word of God commands, not out of legalism, but from a grateful, open heart.
- Submit to authority and learn from those who have learned the hard way.
- Reap the positive benefits in your life.

Dark Reality

- Ignoring the owner's manual can result in confusion about truth and reality and a relativism that results in a less fruitful, less happy life that does not glorify God.
- When we don't submit to God's plan, we miss opportunities to bless others.
- When we do not submit to authority, as his word commands, we harden our consciences and become self-deceived.
- Trusting in ourselves results in pride that places us in opposition to God and makes our lives more difficult.

Reality Discussion Questions

1. Have you ever tried to put something together without consulting the manual? If so, how did it work?

_____

_____

2. According to Scripture, what are God's two supreme commands?

_____

_____

3. How do these two commands about love compare with what you think of when thinking about God's commands?

_____

_____

4. Are there any authorities in your life that you disregard?

_____

_____

5. When have you ignored advice from a friend or family member and paid for it?

_____

_____

6. Explain how all of our choices that ignore authority affect those around us.

_____

_____

7. Explain how all of our choices to honor authority affect those around us.

_____

_____

8. Retake the quiz at the beginning of Real Authority. Did you change any of your answers? Which ones and why?

_____

_____

Prayer

Heavenly Father, thank you that you are not distant from us. Thank you for leaving us your Spirit and an owner's manual to guide our lives. Forgive us for rebelling and going our own way. Help us to understand that it is for our good to follow your ways. Help us to see that you are a loving parent who only wants what is best for us. Give us a willing heart to follow you, and in so doing, bless those around us. In Jesus' name, amen.

SECTION V: MONEY REALITIES

Quiz

Multiple Choice Stories

Choose the *best* answer to the questions below.

1. Matt was finally finished with his teaching degree. He had worked his way through college as an assistant manager at a pizza place, and couldn't wait to find a position as a high school history teacher. After he graduated, he moved out of his apartment into a three bedroom single family home. He also traded in his paid car for a newer one with low payments. He upgraded his cell phone, internet service, and cable service. Matt then gave $1,000 of his graduation gift money as a down payment on his uncle Tom's thirty foot sail boat. His uncle agreed to charge Matt a small, interest-free, monthly payment for the boat. Matt knew this new lifestyle may stretch his budget for a while, but felt he had earned it. The new budget would be comfortable when he acquired a teaching position. And he did have a little more disposable income since he was no longer paying part of his tuition. But when he fell and broke his leg rock climbing, he was surprised by the bill for the $2,000 deductible. Until recently he had been on his parents' medical insurance policy. Unfortunately, Matt didn't have the money for this unexpected expense because he had overextended his budget.

What should Matt do?

 a. He should rework his budget and/or find a roommate to share expenses. He should call the hospital and set up a payment plan for the deductible.

 b. He should call his uncle Tom and see if they could postpone their deal until Matt actually has a new job. He should see if his uncle is willing to refund his deposit and use that to pay part of the deductible.

c. Because he can't pay the bill, he should avoid the phone calls and letters from the hospital. He should not talk to them until he has more money.

d. a and b

2. Lisa, an education major, put an ad on Craigslist about her tutoring services. After a few e-mails with a parent, she began to feel uneasy. The father said he was in Great Britain, but was originally from India. His fifteen year old daughter, Carrie, was returning to live with her Indian nanny in the states to continue her education after spending the summer with him. He explained that the nanny didn't speak English well and had a difficult time with monetary transactions. Carrie's father wanted to send a check for Carrie's tutoring for the entire year along with the nanny's pay. He wanted Lisa to cash the check and pay the nanny her portion in cash. Lisa informed him that she wasn't comfortable with that arrangement, but he insisted.

What should Lisa do?

a. She should accept his check and pay the nanny her portion. Since he is paying for the full year in advance, it is the least she can do.

b. She should insist that he find another way to pay the nanny. If he refuses, she should refuse the business.

3. Melissa's good friend Courtney does not manage her money well. She has a part-time job that helps to supplement her living expenses. Her parents pay for all of her rent, food, utilities, books, and tuition. She is only responsible for her clothing, car insurance, and gas. Every time Courtney's insurance is due, she is short. She asks Melissa for a "loan" and promises to pay her back "soon." Melissa knows it is important for Courtney to maintain her auto insurance, so she helps her friend, only to find her accumulating loan is now up to $300. Melissa is also a student and working only part-time.

What is the best thing Melissa could do for Courtney? She should
_____.

    a.   refuse Courtney the next time she asks for a loan. She would be throwing her money away.

    b.   if Courtney is agreeable, help her set up a budget and an accountability partner, so that she will have enough money to pay her insurance the next time it is due.

    c.   continue to loan her money, so Courtney's insurance won't lapse. It's what friends do.

    d.   insist that Courtney pay back the $300 before she loans her any more money.

TRUE OR FALSE?

Money Realities

True/False 1. Having enough money is the primary ingredient for a happy life.

True/False 2. Christians should not have a lot of wealth.

True/False 3. If you have a low-paying job, you can rightly justify doing personal things at work while you are on the clock.

True/False 4. It is not healthy to identify our personal value with our work title.

True/False 5. Christians should not focus on money.

True/False 6. God is not interested in what we do with our money.

True/False 7. It is smart to use credit cards to build your credit.

True/False 8. If you have debts, it is best to wait until you have the money to contact the debt collector.

True/False 9. A title loan is a great way to get extra money quickly when you have an emergency need.

True/False 10. If you have extra, you should always lend money to friends and family when they ask for it.

13

"Show Me the Money!"[2]

Is Money Evil?

Money is not the culprit. According to Scripture; "the love of money is the root of all evil" (1 Tim. 6:10). Those whose life ambition is to have more money, more stuff, and more power that money brings will never be satisfied. There is always more money to be made, more stuff to accumulate, and more power to gain. Those at the top often continue to clamor for greater heights because money has become their god. Some have sold their soul for money and are still unsatisfied, for money cannot buy lasting happiness.

The accumulation of things may bring pleasure, but it is often short-lived and less satisfying than anticipated. The lives of prominent celebrities can attest to this. Suicides, overdoses, broken relationships and heartache are not foreign to the rich and famous. John Costelloe of the *Sopranos* took his own life. Actor Heath Ledger had just wrapped filming of *The Dark Knight* when he died of a drug overdose. Owen Wilson, actor in *Marley and Me*, *Starsky & Hutch* and numerous other box-office hits, attempted suicide. Elvis died from an overdose and Kurt Cobain of Nirvana shot himself. And the king of pop, Michael Jackson, died a drug related death. Actors Lindsay Lohan and Charlie Sheen have struggled with drug abuse and arrests. The charmed life of professional golfer Tiger Woods proved to be less than charming— multiple affairs and a broken family. The list goes on and on. A glance at the

---

2. Cameron Crowe, *Jerry Maguire*, DVD, Directed by Cameron Crowe, (Gracie Films; Tri-Star Pictures: Culver City, CA, 1996).

daily entertainment news will reveal the latest breakups and lockups of the wealthy and famous. Money does not guarantee happiness.

While money can't deliver lasting happiness, it can relieve some of life's stress. No one will argue that it is satisfying to be able to pay all of our bills on time and have some money left over. When money is in short supply, all of life can take on a sinister darkness. Whether it is from lack of earning enough, unforeseen debt—such as medical bills or careless overspending—a shortage of money can negatively affect your health, emotions and spirit.

Scripture does not condemn having wealth. Many great people in the Bible were wealthy: Abraham, Jacob, David, Solomon, Job, Nicodemus, and Zacchaeus. But those who have accumulated physical wealth are given this admonition, "Command those who are rich in this present world not to be arrogant nor to put their hope in wealth, which is so uncertain, but to put their hope in God, who richly provides us with everything for our enjoyment. Command them to do good, to be rich in good deeds, and to be generous and willing to share. In this way they will lay up treasure for themselves as a firm foundation for the coming age, so that they may take hold of the life that is truly life" (1 Tim. 6:17–19).

It is a great temptation to put our hope in money, rather than in God. Wealth is one of the most universally valued things in the world. Jesus realized its tempting power when he stated, "No servant can serve two masters. Either he will hate the one and love the other, or he will be devoted to the one and despise the other. You cannot serve both God and Money" (Luke 16:13).

We must choose to serve God over money. How would you answer these questions: "What are you living for? How do you spend your time? What are your goals?" These simple questions reveal the focus of your life. Instead of serving money, let money serve you in your service to God.

Money Mirror

Scripture has a lot to say about money and wealth. God understands that in this world, money is essential for living, and it is a great indicator of how mature we are emotionally and spiritually. "For where your treasure is, there your heart will be also" (Matt. 6:21). Where do we spend our money? Do we lavish it on ourselves, or are we generous and giving? Of course, there is a balance in being responsible, paying our bills, and helping to meet others' needs as we are able.

Often we spend without thinking about where our money is going. If you don't live on a budget, money may just seem to disappear. To find out where your money is really going, carefully track your spending for a month. How much do you spend on housing, credit cards, vehicles, groceries, gas, eating out, clothes, giving, saving, investing, entertainment, and, of course, new gizmos, gadgets, and toys! Money mirrors our priorities and reveals what we value. Do you like what you see in your money mirror? If not, you are the one who can change the path you are traveling. A new catch phrase among Christians is to "live on purpose." We should also determine to "spend on purpose."

Work? What's That?

While working as a business manager for many years, I was sadly disappointed in workers who felt that the world owed them a living. Somehow, they felt entitled to a check, regardless of the job they did. I observed many employees who were present in body, but doing non-work related things. They were playing games on the computer, surfing the Internet, doing projects for school, socializing for extended periods, talking on their cell phone, or text messaging.

Of course, most jobs offer necessary breaks and down time to rest, so you can return to work with a better focus on the job at hand. And there are jobs that allow you to do other things if all of your responsibilities are completed. I am not talking about those situations. Nor am I saying you should never have a conversation with a co-worker or never make a personal call (unless company policy prohibits it), but do beware of taking advantage of your employer—especially in unsupervised situations. If you have to hide what you are doing when your boss walks by, you probably shouldn't be doing it!

Those who slack off sometimes use the excuse that they are not being paid as much as they are worth. If you agreed to take the job for the amount you are being paid, you have no excuse. If you are unhappy about your pay, you have a few options. You can find another job, ask for a raise, or realize that you agreed to your current pay and be grateful you have a job. If you feel you are underpaid, the ball is in your court.

I recall a co-worker sitting in her office with a friend all morning, openly working on her resume, on company time. She didn't get it, and she is not alone. Work habits seem to have dropped to the lowest common denominator. Many companies have a policy that you must no show, no call for three days in a row before you are fired. In the past, workers would have lost their job if they failed to show up or to call in with a good explanation even one time. But the quality of workers has declined dramatically, forcing employers to settle for extremely low standards in the work place. Determine to raise the bar and make your boss's day!

Big Brother Is Not Always Watching, but God Is!

Do not be diligent only when your boss is watching; be diligent all the time. The following passage refers to slavery, but the principle applies equally to paid work: "Obey them not only to win their favor when their eye is on you, but like slaves of Christ, doing the will of God from your heart. Serve wholeheartedly, as if you were serving the Lord, not men, because you know that the Lord will reward everyone for whatever good he does, whether he is slave or free" (Eph. 6:6–8). Even if your boss doesn't appreciate your hard work, God does, and he will reward you.

Conscientious work will show in quality and quantity and bring positive benefits into your life. But if you do not fulfill your required responsibilities, you will incur self-inflicted pain. You will more than likely have to deal with unhappy superiors, you may be demoted or lose your job, you may lose self-esteem, or your sloppy work could result in a habit of laziness and, sadly, an unproductive life.

So what are the benefits of having a great work ethic? You likely will be first in line when a promotion comes along. You will gain the respect of your superiors and others you work with. You'll raise the standard so that those without a strong work ethic might improve their job performance, creating a better company and more job stability for you. You will be pleasing God. You will know you are being honest in your job and retain the dignity and self-respect of doing what you know is right. You will have the satisfaction of knowing you are a mature adult, carrying your own weight, rather than being a drain on others. And, over the long term, "Lazy hands make a man poor, but diligent hands bring wealth" (Prov. 10:4).

Don't Overdo It!

**"Don't wear yourself out to get rich; have the
wisdom to show restraint." (Prov. 23:4)**

Ironically, overworking also plagues millions of Americans. While it is crucial to have a good work ethic, working too much can cause great destruction. The desire for more "stuff," prestige, and power can cost health, family, and enjoyment of life. If your family is working to get out of debt, taking a second job or regularly working overtime may be appropriate. Working extra to meet a short-term goal is reasonable and shouldn't cause long-term consequences. But if overworking becomes the norm year after year, the whole family will suffer.

For certain people, work can be addictive. They must make one more phone call, close one more deal, send one more e-mail. It never ends. The work addict rarely shuts down or takes a break. Workaholics become the thirty-five and forty-year-olds who have high blood pressure and heart attacks before their time. Scripture says to have the wisdom to show restraint. It is in our best interest and for our own good to temper the amount of work we do.

Some people tie their self-identity too closely to their level of income and their profession. When a man identifies himself as "an attorney" before he sees himself as John Smith, then he has crossed the line into a false sense of who he is. When your profession becomes your assessment for your value as a person, the tendency toward workaholism probably will surface. It is important to realize that our occupations, like our possessions, are temporary. They don't define us. Occupation is not ultimately who we are. Our character, on the other hand, should be our focus when we think about who we really are. Our hearts are the source of our true being. And the heart can produce a much more rewarding focus than money! "The good man brings good things out of the good stored up in his heart, and the evil man brings evil things out of the evil stored up in his heart" (Luke 6:45).

It is better to never have earthly wealth, but live a life that stores up treasure in heaven, than to bow down to money and career.

Show Some Respect!

As a young person, I didn't have a great respect for money. I knew it was necessary for living, but never gave it much thought or attention beyond what I needed to get by. It was in the background of my life. Work and family were at the forefront (which isn't altogether bad!), but I just didn't care much about money. What I really wanted in life was to make a difference. But just making a difference is not always practical. If we can't feed our families or pay our mortgage, we are shirking on basic responsibilities. Fortunately, when I was in this situation—wanting to and actually making a difference, but not making much money—extended family came to the rescue. They stepped in where it really wasn't their responsibility. Life would have been so much easier had I given money a little more attention.

Scripture mentions money 114 times and wealth 124 times. We should consider and plan our financial resources carefully. For many people this is not a problem, but for the ministry-minded or artistically inclined, money is sometimes underestimated in regard to its true importance. Many a missionary has retired broke, completely dependent on friends and family or the government. While money shouldn't be an end in itself, it can certainly make life simpler and make contributing to the needs of others possible. So don't allow money to fade into the background; make financial goals that ultimately will help you achieve adequate support of your family and enable you to generously reach out to worthy ministries and those in need.

One of the greatest errors I have made in this area was to undercut myself financially. When I was in business, I offered a service and product that helped people, but significantly undercharged for what the market could bear at the time. After I sold the business, but continued to manage it, the new owner more than doubled the prices, and the company's sales did not decrease. In fact, I was still the primary sales person; I still believed in the service and saw no change in my closing ratio. Had I more clearly valued money and raised the prices myself, I may have been able to survive without selling the business.

Another area to manage wisely is compensation for a job. Formerly, when I worked for other people, I always took the salary they offered, never negotiating for the best deal. I had excellent experience, education, and references and was really in a position to bargain, but I never did because I didn't appropriately value money. At one particular job, I accepted the first offer and later discovered from other employees that the position had been advertised on the Internet for 25 percent more! Unfortunately, I saw it in the newspaper, where a salary wasn't listed. Evidently, this businessman had expected to negotiate. If you are worth more, ask for more. That is being a good steward of your talents, time, and energy.

Taking Care of Business

While most of us don't see ourselves as taking care of business when we spend money, we are actually acting as stewards (managers). Everything we have is God's. He has entrusted us with life, health, talents, and money. Some have more than others, but we are accountable only for what he has entrusted to us. Whether you have a little or a lot of money, you must be aware that you are accountable for how it is spent. It has been said that the eye is the window to the soul. I'd like to offer an alternate adage. Your money is the window to your soul.

In the parable of the talents (Matt. 25:14–29), Jesus teaches that we must be good stewards of what we have. When we do not watch how our money is spent, we can squander it, be irresponsible with it, or consume it all on our own wants. God has provided us with means to make money so that we can be responsible, meeting our needs and the needs of our family, and use it to help those who are less fortunate. God is not against wealth, he just wants us to be wise in how we use what he has given us. It doesn't mean we should never buy something we want rather than need. It just means we should be aware of where our money is going. Are we giving a portion to God and using the rest wisely? Would God be pleased with what we have done with his money?

At a recent disaster-relief seminar, I saw a video about the demographics of the world if it were condensed down to one hundred people. The statistics are alarming and sad. I found several similar videos on YouTube (Global Village, Miniature Earth) and compared other statistics from various atlases and United Nations sources, and they are all fairly close: If the world were comprised of one hundred people and the world's total wealth were $100, then six people would own $59, seventy-four would own $39, and twenty people would share the remaining $2. Of the one hundred, only eight would have money in the bank. Those twenty living in poverty would have inadequate housing, insufficient food, unclean water and unsanitary living conditions. That is one out of every five in the world! Of the one hundred, only seven would own a car (some of the seven would own more than one). Only twelve would have a computer, and only three would have Internet service. Just one of the hundred would have a university-level education, and at least fifteen would be illiterate. Various sources had slightly different statistics, but no matter which source you look at, the conclusion is the same. Americans are overwhelmingly blessed, financially and otherwise.

If you have not traveled outside the United States, you may not realize how truly wealthy you are. Looking at the statistics above, we should be grateful for our abundance. And we need to be good stewards of all we've been entrusted. "From everyone who has been given much, much will be demanded; and from the one who has been entrusted with much, much more will be asked" (Luke 12:48). May God help us to be faithful with our finances.

Part of being a good steward is to take care of the things you have bought. If you are careless with your belongings, either losing, failing to maintain them, or destroying them, you will have to spend additional money replacing them, or you will have to go without. You honor God when you take care of your stuff! "The diligent man prizes his possessions" (Prov. 12:27).

Enough Is Enough

What is enough? Every person has grown up with a particular socio-economic status, and often we try to live at that standard when we launch out on our own. Most often it took our parents several decades to achieve their financial status. But it is not uncommon for children to want to have everything their parents have accumulated over twenty-five years as soon as they move out. This unrealistic expectation can lead to financial disaster.

It is not bad to have financial goals or a desire to have the nice things our parents have or even more than they have. But it is not reasonable to think that we will be able to attain that level immediately when we move out on our own. It took them years; it could take us years. Don't get sucked into the buy now, pay later mentality of buying on credit. While it may work for awhile, it can snowball into an avalanche of debt and destruction.

If your spending is greater than your income, think about what things are necessities and distinguish that from what you may want. Global necessities are shelter, food, clothes, and transportation to get to work. Of course, transportation may mean having access to a bus, train, or subway, not necessarily owning a vehicle yourself. In comparison to much of the world, having these basics make us quite wealthy.

Many things we consider necessities are actually luxuries or at least extras over what we need to live comfortably. Can you live without your iPhone, digital cable, high-speed Internet access, eating out, Starbucks, and name-brand clothes? What is on your list of extras? If these extras are breaking your budget, ask God to help you to know what enough is and how to live within your means. Resolve to make changes when you discover areas where you can cut back.

We should always be grateful for the opportunity to live in a country where we can advance our careers, incomes, and lifestyles, and be good stewards with what we've been entrusted. We should be mindful of others as our incomes and lifestyles increase, rather than just increasing our "stuff." God created a world full of resources for wealth. He is not against wealth; he just wants us to be generous with our income and not consume all of it on ourselves.

14

Do's and *Don'ts*

Don't Do Debt

Our stewardship of money mandates discipline. To commit to spending more than we bring in is self-destructive. Thousands of Americans are imploding because they are deeply in debt, regularly spending more than they earn. The Center for American Progress reports that the average American spends 129 percent of disposable income, which means the average American is in debt, spending more than they are making.

David Ramsey says consumer debt increased from $1.4 trillion to about $11.5 trillion between 1980 and 2005. Ramsey has gained much wisdom about managing money. He explains that his greatest lessons are not from his college degree, but from learning the hard way, by grossly mismanaging his finances. Now his mission is to help others to stay on track in order to glorify God with the material wealth with which they have been entrusted. Dave Ramsey's *Financial Peace* and *The Total Money Makeover* offer in-depth practical insights. Those who can learn from others' mistakes are truly wise and will avoid much sorrow.

Some financial experts recommend against having credit cards, period. The temptation is too great to use them. If you are maxed out at the end of the week or month (or however often you get paid), I would agree with them. The temptation may be too great to use them. Learn to live within your means. Cut up your credit cards. That is one sure way you won't use them again!

On the other hand, if you have substantial disposable income and by having a particular store credit card, you get a 15 percent to 50 percent discount every time you shop there, use it wisely and pay it off every month, so that you never pay interest on it. But if you can't pay it off completely every month, don't use it. Better yet, cut it up. If you don't pay it off each month, that discount will quickly be eaten up in interest and fees. And if you end up making late payments, it will also hurt your credit score. Most mortgage companies use your credit score as a primary criterion when you buy a house. Don't mess that up by buying stuff that is beyond your "enough."

Don't Ignore Debt

If you're already in over your head, there are some things you can do to make a bad situation tolerable.

The most important thing is what not to do. Don't ignore debt. It won't go away on its own. Make it a financial priority to get out of debt as quickly as possible. Allowing debt fees and interest to accrue will only make the hole deeper and more difficult to climb out. When we feel overwhelmed and unable to pay, it is natural to want to run and hide—ignoring calls and letters. Don't give in to that temptation. It will cost more financially and emotionally in the end. Denial is actually a form of lying to ourselves. If I don't deal with it, it doesn't exist. Wrong. If I don't deal with it, it gets worse. Those in denial eventually crash and sometimes burn when reality breaks through. And it is just a matter of time.

Consider taking on a part-time job or working overtime for a while as a remedy for accumulated debt. Jobs waiting tables or delivering pizza don't require any special skills or extended training. Both pay an hourly wage plus tips, and these jobs are usually plentiful. Or, if you have other talents or training to make extra money quickly, use those for a quick boost to your income. Utilize what you have to make what you need to get out of debt, but don't start up a new business that will put you further in the red in an effort get out of debt.

Another way to conquer debt is to cut back on your current lifestyle for a time and put the money saved toward the debt. If you golf once a week, cut back to once a month. If you usually vacation for two weeks, cut back to one week this year. Even small things like cutting your daily

Starbucks fix can add up. So start making coffee at home. You'll be amazed at how much money you save. Decide which extras in your life you can do without for a time. Make a list and plan to do without those pleasures until you are out of debt.

Dave Ramsey suggests a process called debt snowball as an efficient way to pay off debt. Several years ago I used this system to eliminate debt. It proved to be an efficient way to rid myself of the weight of indebtedness. List your debt from the smallest to the largest (total amount, not payment amount). Work on paying off the smallest debt first. Any extra money you earn or save should go toward the smallest debt, regardless of interest. Then when that is paid off, take the money you would have used to pay that debt and any other extra money coming in to go toward the next smallest debt, etc. This method helps you to see results the fastest and frees up additional money quickly to go toward other debt. Persevering is easier when you see results on a regular basis. So stop the debt accumulation snowball and start the debt relief snowball today.

Handling Debt Collectors

If you are receiving calls from a creditor, don't allow them to abuse you. They are not permitted to call before 8 a.m., after 9 p.m., or to call you at work if you tell them you are not to be contacted at work. If they are threatening to harm you, your reputation or your property—or if they use obscene or profane language or are calling and repeatedly harassing you—hang up the phone. According to the Fair Debt Collection Practices Act, debt collectors do not have a right to abuse you by engaging in any of these practices.

Be reasonable and honest with the bill collector—only make arrangements that you will be able to keep. Offering to make small regular payments is better than no payments. Often they will agree to stop fees and interest if you have a plan to pay off your debt. Don't avoid calls or letters. They will not go away. Fees and interest will accrue, and your debt may be handed over to a collection agency. Collection agencies are typically more aggressive in their collection practices than are the companies that hire them.

Do not allow a collection agency to mistreat you either. The Federal Debt Collection Practices Act prohibits "deceptive, unfair and abusive" practices by third-party collectors. If they refuse to stop harassing you, you have the right to send the collector written notice to cease communications regarding the debt. Just realize that fees and interest don't stop accruing while they are not contacting you. If it is a legitimate debt, you still owe it.

Many companies, particularly collection agencies, will agree to a settlement for a percentage of what you owe. If you find you just cannot come up with the full amount, make an offer. Often they will agree to anywhere from 30 percent to 80 percent of what you owe. Make sure you have the agreement in writing before you pay and then written confirmation of payment, so that they cannot come back later and claim that you still owe them money. If they do not send confirmation right away, keep calling until you have it in hand. Do not throw it away, ever! Companies have been known to come back years later and claim clients owe them money. Protect yourself and keep proof of payment.

Also keep copies of all taxes paid—property, personal property, local, and federal. Ten years after I paid personal property tax on a car, I received a bill for that tax I had already paid! I was extremely glad I still had the receipt. Taxes are high enough without paying them twice.

Do Live Within Your Means, Not Your Wants

Many people see a home they want to live in and then stretch their financial resources to make that a reality, rather than living within their means. They become "house poor." I have known a number of people who decided that having the house of their dreams and the brand-new vehicle they wanted was more important than anything else, and it usually ended in financial disaster. All of their money was going into that perfect home and car they had to have, and they had little left to live on, especially when extra expenses surfaced, or they lost a job.

For most of my life, when money came in, I found a place for it to go out. I never accumulated a savings or emergency account, and typically lived in the best home and drove the best car I thought I could afford—which was never extravagant, but possibly more than I should have bought. I was usually maxed out. I never had much extra and at times was at a deficit when unexpected expenses arose. Life is stressful when there is more month than money. Not maxing out your budget allows you to have a buffer in your financial life, which helps to keep your emotional life more stable as well.

You can count on unexpected expenses. The car will break down, the dog or kids will get sick, the roof will leak, gas prices will soar, or some other unforeseen event will cause you to need extra money. If your budget assigns all of your money for bills and living, with little or no extra, you'll be in trouble when a crisis hits. And when it comes time for birthdays, graduations, weddings, Christmas, and vacations, it will be tempting to use credit cards instead of cash. Plan ahead financially for the unexpected. It is coming.

Don't Overdraw

Try to keep at least a $100 buffer in your checking account. When you are working from your online balance, you must consider checks that haven't cleared and charges from debit cards that haven't gone through. Most debit charges show immediately, but sometimes it can take a few days to go through. Using your online balance as a guideline to know how much is left is dangerous. It may eventually come back to bite you.

James accidently overdrew his account and ended up paying several hundred dollars because of his mistake. By just looking at his balance online, he thought he had $35 more than he actually had. His gas charge from the day before wasn't showing, but he didn't notice. So he bought several small things on his debit card—two candy bars from the convenience store and a bag of ice from the corner supermarket. The next day he bought a coffee from McDonald's, deodorant from Wal-Mart, and a few days later a meal from Taco Bell. He accumulated five overdrafts from the bank at a fee of $30 each. The kicker was that his bank continued to charge an additional $8 daily as long as his account was overdrawn.

James had moved, so the overdraft notices didn't reach him for almost two weeks, and by then things had snowballed. On his first set of overdrafts James accrued $280 worth of charges on about $20 worth of goods. When his $550 pay check went in, more than half of it was already gone. But he was unaware and paid a few bills without looking at his balance, overdrawing the account again. When he finally looked at his account online, he was $352 in the red. He had made several small purchases again after his two larger bills, and each one was charged $30 for an overdraft. It was a hard lesson to learn. When James called the bank, the manager agreed to cancel half of the overdraft charges, because those were his first overdrafts, but he told James they wouldn't reduce overdraft charges again. James now tells his horror story to his friends, "I paid $50 for a candy bar!" That is a kind of inflation you should avoid.

If it is available from your bank, sign up for an alert via e-mail or text message when your account falls below a certain amount. Even when that is set up, it is still your responsibility to balance your account, because banks make mistakes too!

15

Cons, Get-Rich-Quick Schemes, and Bad Ideas

The old adage "if it sounds too good to be true, it probably is" is worth digesting. Scams are found in abundance and have all sorts of faces and angles. Some guidelines, common cons, and plain old bad ideas are listed below.

Free Services/Products

If an ad says their service or product is free, read the small print. Free credit reports, free songs from iTunes, and other "freebies" often turn into ongoing monthly charges after the initial free service or product. They automatically deduct the fee from your account. If the ad asks for credit card or banking information, consider that a red flag and read the fine print. While these aren't necessarily a con, they can be misleading. When you read the entire document, you'll find there are ongoing fees after a "free trial" period. If you fail to read the fine print and accept the "free service/product," your money may unexpectedly disappear out of your account, leaving you short.

Check In the Mail

Don't cash an unexpected check you receive in the mail without reading the fine print. By cashing it, you may be giving the company permission to change your phone service or enroll you in an ongoing travel or insurance service, which will come with fees after a thirty-day trial. Or, worse yet, you may inadvertently be giving them access to your account.

Multi-Level Marketing (MLM)

While many legitimate companies operate on a multi-level basis, most people fail to make enough to live on in multi-level marketing. I have joined a few MLM companies over the years (Amway, Mary Kay, and Xango) and even still use some of their products, but I never made any substantial money and was never able to quit my day job. Many of my friends and family have done the same thing, signing up and then petering out when significant money wasn't forthcoming. You'll hear about exceptions in the MLM sales pitch. Some people do become wealthy in MLM, or at least make a living. If you are a strongly driven individual with a large network of friends and family to whom you wouldn't mind selling, it may be viable for you. Just make sure you build your business to a point where it can support you before quitting your salaried job.

Loans with Outrageous Interest

Almost weekly I receive a check in the mail—a loan for which I haven't applied. These are from legal companies who want to lend me money. Usually they have outrageous interest—the last one I received was 38 percent! Don't ever give in to "easy" money. If you make the minimum payments, you could spend years if not decades repaying such a loan and will have paid several times what you borrowed by the time it is paid off.

Car Title Loans

Don't do it! They can charge insane interest annually. In the June 22, 2008, edition of the Chicago Tribune, Stephen Franklin reported that one Kansas company was charging 460 percent annually on title loans (using the loophole of revolving credit) before reducing the rate to 300 percent when pressured by the state. Often, title companies list the interest in monthly terms to make it sound cheaper. The annual interest for a 25 percent a month loan is 300 percent. Oregon, Florida, Kentucky, and Iowa have enforced lower caps on title loans, but they still allow fairly high interest rates. Every month, title loan companies repossess cars because the borrowers can't repay.

Arial borrowed $1,000 against her car at 25 percent monthly and planned to repay it within a year. When she couldn't make her payments, she negotiated a lower amount that didn't cover all of the interest. After a year of making payments, she owed over $2,000. Her budget wouldn't allow a higher payment, so every month she was going further into debt. Eventually her car was repossessed.

I called a local title loan company and in the course of the conversation asked several times for their interest rate. They refused to tell me. I was told their interest is half of their competitors; I wasn't told what their competitor's rate was. If they won't tell you the interest rate on the phone, don't waste your time going by their office. They may be legal, but they shouldn't be.

Private Information Requests

Never give your social security, credit/debit card or bank account numbers to anyone you haven't contacted. If someone calls or e-mails and says they are with a business with which you have an account and asks for this information for any reason, do not give it out. Give it only to someone with whom you have initiated contact. People can say they are with anyone, and if they are asking for your personal information, it is not likely that they are really with that company.

Financial Institution Fraud

Sometimes scammers disguise e-mails to look like they are from financial institutions, possibly even one you do business with. If they request personal information, do not give it. If it is your bank, call and tell them about the e-mail. Your financial institution will not send an e-mail requesting your account or social security number. They already have them.

Pay for Prize

Never pay to receive a prize, gift, tax grant, or award (or a job!). If you have to pay for your prize or pay a processing fee up front (even if they claim it is refundable), the offer is more than likely a scam. We regularly get announcements in the mail, through e-mail, and on the phone that we have won one of several prizes, but first we must pay for tax or shipping or something up front. If you do decide to pay and in fact do receive a prize, it may be a cheap product worth less than what you paid.

Overseas Fraud

Never "help" a person overseas by cashing a check or using your account to deposit their money. Several variety of scams have come from Nigeria and other countries with the person claiming to be a political or bank official, writing about an overpayment on a procurement contract, a sales contract, a credit card, a religious-based contribution, an inheritance, or claiming to be someone who wants to buy your inventory or invest in your company. They usually want an up-front fee and promise you money down the road. They sometimes ask for your social security number and bank account number. Don't do it!

Lottery Winner

Another version of overseas fraud informs you that you have won the lottery. Sometimes these international scams are very sophisticated and look legitimate. We received a $4,900 "advance on winning" check from "Chase Bank" through a Canadian company for winning an Australian lottery we never entered. It was a scam. The letter said they sent the check so that we could pay the $2,900 tax (they wanted it sent Western Union to Canada) on the $750,000 winning. That would leave an extra $2,000 for us immediately. If we had deposited the check and then wired the money, we would not be up $2,000. We'd be down $2,900 because the check was fake—although it looked very real. By the time the check bounced, the scam artists would have their money, and we'd never hear from them again. Remember, if you are promised a large sum of money as payment for your help or to pay a tax or fee, it is a scam. Don't let the prospect of a large amount of money blind you.

Exceptional Return

If someone offers you an unbelievable return on your money, don't fall for it—many schemes promise 40 percent or more. Cons prey on our natural greed and desire to get rich quickly. They use a variety of investments— money trading, real estate projects, certificates of deposit, stocks, or other investments that sound promising. Typically they will send an incredible return to the first investors by using future investor's money. These first investors often reinvest their returns and tell friends and family, who in turn invest their money. Typically, after the scam artist has collected several million dollars, he disappears with everyone's money, and there are no more returns and almost no recovery of the invested money. On occasion a small percentage is retrieved, but most often it is gone forever.

Fortunately such con men are sometimes caught. Most well known is Bernard Madoff who conducted such a Ponzi scheme, bilking investors out of $18 billion. He carried on this scheme for at least fifteen years, and when it finally ran out of money, he confessed to his sons who turned him in. He is now serving a 150 year sentence.

There are endless variations on this type of scam, even those who profess to be Christians. In recent news is a story about three men who claimed divine intervention in their financial ruin. They went to homes and churches across North Carolina and South Carolina, telling their story. These three convinced 7,000 investors from two dozen states to hand over $80 million for investment in foreign currencies exchanges "that banks kept secret." Less than $40,000 was actually invested. The men bought a $5 million jet, twenty cars and trucks, real estate, and a $180,000 luxury box at a sports arena. The courts found and froze accounts containing only $17 million.

These men went to church together and named their enterprise "3 Hebrew Boys" for the biblical story of three Hebrews who, because of their faith, survived unscathed through the fiery furnace (see Dan. 3). The 3 Hebrew Boys' clients were mainly believers and military base residents. They targeted those in similar affinity groups, as is often the case, and enlisted respected pastors, deacons, and retired soldiers to unwittingly help them propagate their scam. They promised 200 to 500 percent daily return and used money from new investors to pay earlier investors to veil the deception. The FBI estimates that they were within months of collapse when their assets were frozen. Unlike many accused of fraud, these three men didn't flee the country or disappear. They were caught and have been found guilty of mail fraud, money laundering, and transporting stolen goods. They were sentenced to decades in prison and were ordered to pay $82 million in restitution. Only $20 million has been recovered, so those bilked will receive just a small percentage of their money back.

Own Business

The Internet is filled with offers to own your own business or run a business from home. Hundreds of scams offer you full-time pay or six-figure incomes for very little investment of your time and sometimes a small amount of seed money. For example, they promise that it will only cost $1,000 to make $100,000 a year working ten hours a week. Or you can make $1,000 an hour working from home if you just send them a small fee. Don't count on it. Again, if it sounds too good to be true, it is.

Any Means

These scams can arrive via fax, phone, e-mail, text or the Internet. Don't fall prey and lose your hard-earned money to a liar. Don't suffer unnecessarily by falling for a scam.

16

Money Habits of Successful People

Give Cheerfully

That sounds like quite an order, but is not difficult when we have an accurate perspective of reality. God wants us to tithe happily (giving back to God the first 10 percent of what he has given to us). While we are to be a good steward of all our resources, tithing reminds us where our income ultimately originates—he has given us our gifts, talents, abilities, strength, and even our very life. And he asks us to give only a small portion back to him—cheerfully. When we recognize that it is all his already, and we are being entrusted with it, we can give gladly.

When we think we are the originator of our resources, or that we have to give to earn favor with God, that is when we give grudgingly. "Each man should give what he has decided in his heart to give, not reluctantly or under compulsion, for God loves a cheerful giver" (2 Cor. 9:7). God does not want us giving out of legalistic compulsion, thinking we are making brownie points with him. He wants us to give out of gratefulness for a multitude of blessings we enjoy, part of which is financial.

From a practical standpoint, tithing supports our churches and ministries, which spread the gospel and help those around us. Many involved in full-time ministerial service rely on the tithes of others for their living. It is right and just for us to support those involved in our spiritual growth and development. "The worker deserves his wages" (Luke 10:7). We don't expect the contractor to build our home without being paid. Nor should we expect those involved in full-time ministry to serve for free. In spite of this reality, many ministers are of necessity bi-vocational, needing other jobs to support their families; their reward for their sacrifices will be great in heaven.

Can You Give too Much?

A few years ago, while attending a Bible study, I had an "aha!" moment as a seemingly contradictory verse was explained. Galatians 6:2 says, "Carry each other's burdens, and in this way you will fulfill the law of Christ." Verse 5 goes on to say, "for each one should carry his own load."

The "burden" in this passage indicates an overwhelming, crushing weight. It is more than what one person can easily handle alone. We should go alongside the person carrying the great burden and offer support and help, be it financial, physical, or emotional. When a tornado blows our home away, a family member passes away, we go through a divorce, or we are dealing with a serious illness in the family, we have "burdens."

The "load" mentioned in verse 5 indicates our own responsibilities—our jobs, schools, or relationships. But when we get up in the morning, go to school or work, handle our daily tasks, pay our bills, and meet our obligations, these things are our personal load. We should not place this load on someone else to carry. If we do, we may overburden them by not carrying our fair share of life's responsibilities. We should not be totally dependent on others, nor should we be totally independent from others. A balance exists where everyone is carrying his own load, and all are chipping in to carry burdens. It is a beautiful example of expressing God's love.

Of course, when family and friends need help, and it is within our means to help, we should lend a hand if: (1) It would not create an enabling situation where he is being encouraged to be habitually dependant rather than personally independent. (2) It will not enable him to continue making poor decisions (addictions, laziness, etc.). (3) It will not keep the helper from meeting his obligations. If helping another pay his bills will keep us from paying ours, we are giving more than we should.

It is not wrong to give financial help to others as long as we are not stifling their spiritual and emotional growth. As is often the case, we must find a balance to our generosity and helpfulness to friends and family. You will probably discover that there will be times in your life when you receive financial blessing from others and times when you give that blessing to others. That is as it should be.

Budget

The first step to tracking and using your money wisely is to make a budget. After taking out a tenth for God, write down how much you bring in and how much you will spend on your essential bills: housing, utilities, food, gas (leave room for inflation). Many recommend that your housing expense should not exceed 25 percent to 30 percent of your take-home pay. If you find that you are spending more than that, you should think about making a change in either your living situation or your job. Find something cheaper to rent/own or find a job with a higher income or a second job. Write down other regular expenditures—such as utilities, food, gas, insurance, car payment, tuition, revolving credit, cell phone, and cable.

Know where your money is going. This is the first step to managing your money. Make adjustments where needed. If you need to reduce your spending on clothes, then do it. Buying clearance items can save hundreds of dollars a year. You can still buy what you want, just buy it off season. Or you may need to stop taking so many road trips. Enjoy what your local community has to offer. Often, people travel hundreds of miles for vacation and tourism, but haven't explored their local attractions. You can also save on utilities. Keep your thermostat a little higher in the summer and a little lower in the winter. Adjust your wardrobe for comfort rather than your thermostat. If you are a movie buff and often pay to see every great movie the day it is released, wait until it comes out on DVD and rent it, or if you have pay per view on cable, watch it there instead of paying a much higher price at the theater. Numerous strategies for saving money exist if you are willing to put together a plan and sacrifice a little. Then get the whole family on board and live on your budget without forfeiting your financial future for what you want today.

Save

Part of being a good steward is to save money for emergencies and large purchases. Emergencies happen. You may lose your glasses, have a tooth ache, blow an engine, or the computer you are using for school might crash. If you don't have an emergency fund, the temptation is to use credit to take care of the situation. With high interest rates you end up paying much more for these things than if you had paid cash. We are not being good stewards of God's money when we pay a lot of interest. Build up an emergency fund of $1,500. When you use it, replenish it as soon as possible.

If you are not in debt, saving 5 percent to 10 percent of what you earn is a good habit to create. Put it in the budget. Then when you want to purchase that new 52-inch plasma TV, you won't be tempted to buy it on credit. You'll have the money set aside to pay cash. Vacations and holidays won't put you further in the hole. And when you are ready to buy a home, you'll have the down payment set aside. If you are very frugal, diligent and patient, you could even pay for your home with cash!

Invest

Eventually, if we should live to a reasonably old age, most of us will retire. That may seem like an eternity from now, but it will arrive sooner than you can imagine! So it is important that part of your current income be invested for retirement. Average inflation is about 3 percent to 4 percent a year, so if you just save without investing, you'll be losing the buying power of your money. Retirement funds should be set aside, where they are not easy to access. A 401(k) is available through most companies, and if you are self-employed, you can invest for retirement through Simplified Employee Pension Plan (SEPP). Check with your accountant or Mutual Fund Broker for more details. This money can be set aside tax free and will grow through safe investments. For the safest return, many financial advisors recommend mutual funds with a good long-term record.

With the recent upheaval in the stock market, investing in anything where losing your investment is possible may be more risk than you want to take. Certificates of Deposit (CDs) with a small return are available at your bank and are completely safe. That will at least keep inflation from robbing the value of your savings. After the required term, you will receive the interest promised. Currently, banks are insured by the FDIC for up to $250,000 per account holder.

Being a good steward includes making a return on the excess money you have been entrusted. Then you will be able to freely give of your financial blessings to others and provide for retirement.

For more details on budgeting and investing see David Ramsey's books *Financial Peace* and *The Total Money Makeover*. He includes helpful worksheets to track your money—income, expenditures, debts, and investments. We should adjust our financial goals as life progresses and changes. Taking any steps in the right direction can make a long-term difference, so start making small changes today and you will be on the road to better financial health. Gradually incorporate all of these principles and gain financial freedom.

Since I started appreciating the value of money somewhat late in life, I have yet to achieve all of my financial goals, but I am working on them and continue to learn and experience that abiding by sound financial principles makes life much easier and costs less in soul toll.

SECTION V: MONEY REALITIES

OVERVIEW

Summary

The way we use money reflects our soul and reveals our priorities. We must consider that all we have is from God, and we are stewards of the finances he has entrusted to us. We should not love money, but we should respect it as a necessary and important part of life. We should not wear ourselves out to become wealthy, making money our god. Living within our means is essential, and we should watch for common pitfalls such as getting into consumer debt, maxing out our budget, overdrawing our accounts, and becoming subject to cons and bad financial decisions. In today's communication-accessible society scams and schemes are abundant. Mail, Internet, faxes, and phones open doors for a con to walk into your life. (Sometimes cons even use church as an avenue.) Be on guard. We should develop a right perspective and good habits, so that we can give cheerfully, budget, save, and invest with God's help and wisdom.

Light Reality

- Keeping a balanced view of work and finances in our lives will enable us to live debt free and unencumbered by the woes of those who either work or spend too much, focusing on the physical rather than spiritual realities.
- Cheerfully giving 10 percent (or more) will help us remember that all we have is from God, and we are willing grateful stewards of what he has entrusted to us.
- Developing positive money habits allows us to gain the peace of financial stability and the joy of being able to give generously.

Dark Reality

• Making money our god will keep us from seeing the reality of life from a spiritual perspective. We will accumulate and enviously want more without ever being satisfied.

• Selfishly consuming all we have on ourselves will blind us to the needs of those around us.

• Failing to make and take a course of action with our finances results in irresponsibility and suffering the woes of financial strain.

• When we do not wisely use what God has entrusted to us, we will not accomplish all the good works he has planned for us, and we will short circuit much joy that comes from giving.

"For where your treasure is, there your heart will be also." (Matt. 6:21)

Reality Discussion Questions

1. My main attitude toward money is

_____

_____

2. After observing my money for a month, my money mirror tells me my priorities are

_____

_____

3. How I feel about my priorities:

_____

_____

4. If I am not happy with my money mirror, I will

_____

_____

5. My worst money bad habit is

_____

_____

6. This month I will change that by doing what?

_____

_____

7. A new positive money habit from chapter 16 that I haven't previously practiced is _____. This month I will change that by doing what?

_____

_____

8. Retake the quiz at the beginning of Money Realities. Did you change any of your answers? Which ones and why?

_____

_____

Prayer

Heavenly Father, help me to view money as you do. Thank you for the gifts and talents you have given me that enable me to earn a living. Give me wisdom and discipline to use my money for your glory. Forgive me for past poor money choices and attitudes. Today, help me to see one area where I can change my money habits. Give me strength to follow through and continue to help me to grow in this area. In Jesus' name, amen.

SECTION VI: LIFESTYLE REALITIES

Quiz

Multiple Choice Stories

Choose the *best* answer to the questions below.

1. After high school graduation, Bill spent a year at a private college upstate, but none of his closest friends, Steven, Zach, or James, continued their education. When he returned home the first summer, he found they had split up. James was no longer hanging out with Steven and Zach. According to James, Steven and Zach started to get into trouble after Bill left town. In the first incident, Steven was arrested for drunk driving and Zach for assaulting the officer when they were stopped. After that Steven and Zach had been in and out of the county jail several times on drug, assault, and theft charges. Zach's dad, an attorney, has kept them out of prison thus far. When Bill met with Steven and Zach, they glossed over the incidents as "no big deal;" there had been a series of "misunderstandings." Both were on parole and doing community service. But, if they had another strike against them, they would serve time in the state penitentiary. Steven and Zach accuse James of being a snob, thinking he is too good for them. And James is fed up with Steven and Zach's poor behavior. Bill is caught in the middle.

What should Bill do?

    a. He should take James' side and avoid hanging out with Steven and Zach. Steven and Zach will get the message when he avoids them and no longer takes their calls.

b. He should take Steven and Zach's side and not hang out with James. Jesus came for sinners and Steven and Zach are prime candidates for redemption.

c. He should stop hanging out with all of his old friends; that way he won't have to take sides.

d. He should tell each of the three that he values their friendship. And he should let Steven and Zach know that if they are involved in anything illegal, he will have no part of it. Knowing their recent history, Bill should be on guard when he is with them.

2. Jennifer, a single woman, works as a business consultant for a large group of radio stations. She enjoys the variety in her responsibilities and has made some great friends with similar interests. The manager of the group, Craig, is a married man with small children. Jennifer and Craig hit it off immediately. Craig is a take charge personality, and Jennifer is drawn to his confidence. Jennifer has a keen business mind, so Craig respects her opinion. Over time their relationship has progressed from colleagues to something more. At first it was just a lunch out occasionally. And then it was a weekly dinner after work. She hadn't intended to, but Jennifer had allowed feelings for Craig to grow. Yesterday, when Jennifer was in Craig's office, he locked the door and started to make a move. She panicked, unlocked the door, and ran out of the office.

What should she do?

a. She should move to another city and start her career over.

b. She should go with the flow. They are both adults. Finding true love is rare, and it may never come along again.

c. She should ask her friends at the office for advice. They know Craig well and could offer their insights.

d. She should suggest another consultant for the group and decline to do any more consulting for them. Jennifer should be more cautious in the future by guarding her heart and mind.

TRUE OR FALSE?

Lifestyle Realities

True/False 1. We should not plan for the future, but just take one day at a time.

True/False 2. You should be friends with everyone you are in contact with.

True/False 3. Eating habits, exercise, and sleep patterns do not affect your spiritual well-being.

True/False 4. The entertainment we enjoy does not affect our spiritual life.

True/False 5. It is not possible to give or do too much for someone we love.

True/False 6. There are rigid rules that determine what content we should watch on TV or in movies and what we should read in books.

True/False 7. The best way to avoid evil is to join a monastery.

True/False 8. Since God is love, he does not hate anything.

True/False 9. Even strong Christians sometimes succumb to temptation.

True/False 10. Innocent flirting never hurt anyone.

17

What You Feed Grows;
What You Starve Dies

As a freshman in college, I was required to take a class called Personal &
Social Adjustment. Professor Miller repeated a phrase regularly in class.
"What you feed grows; what you starve dies." It became the class mantra
and was often heard outside the walls of the classroom. In and of itself, it
sounds obvious, trivial, and unimpressive. But it is, in fact, profound and
applies to all of life.

An opposing, but prevalent view is that "everything happens for a
reason; it's meant to be." This can be a fatalistic approach that absolves
individuals from responsibility when they choose the bad and starve the
good things in their life. Just because it happens, doesn't mean it was
meant to be or God ordained. To suggest such a philosophy would indicate
that all men do God's will. If it were so, we would have heaven on earth.
Unfortunately, that is not the case.

Growing = Life

I watched God paint a sunrise over the ocean this morning. It was gor-
geous—reds, yellows, purples, and blues, with white tips on each cloud.
It was ever-changing, ever-growing, and ever more beautiful. That is how
God works with us. He does not want us to be stagnant, with the same old
problems, issues, and unhealthy responses and lifestyles. He wants us pli-
able, soft, and able to grow and change. Of course, if we are not deliberate

in the choices we make, we can grow in the wrong direction, becoming bitter, angry and full of ugly things as well.

Every day you paint the picture of your future, one stroke at a time. When you make good, wise choices, the future is magnificent, like a stunning sunrise. When you make bad decisions, you paint dark, gloomy strokes, making your future bleak, stormy, and unpleasant. None of us make all wise or all foolish choices. When you are following God, you are not the only one painting your future. You paint a stroke, and God paints a stroke. You paint a stroke, and God paints a stroke. And he is quite the artist! His strokes can cover over the poor choices you have made and recreate your future so that it is amazing (see Jer. 18:4). We must accept the consequences of our choices, but we can be changed into a different, better person with an awesome future if we allow God to paint with us.

All of us have areas in which we need positive growth. To believe we have arrived in every part of our life means we are not delving very deeply into the word or not looking very closely at ourselves. With God's word as a measure, our imperfections become crystal clear. But God's grace and mercy extend to our shortcomings, and he is our greatest cheerleader, encouraging us to move beyond where we find ourselves, and into a greater measure of light and love. If we stagnate, we miss out on so much of God's goodness that could bless our lives and bring him glory.

Life includes growth in every category—emotional, spiritual, physical, and mental. We make choices every day to grow, stagnate, or decline in each of these areas. Life does not just happen to us. While many things are out of our control, much of our life is the direct result of choices we have made. We hold the keys to avoiding much darkness. If we follow God's directions, life will be much easier.

What you feed grows; what you starve dies.

Choose Friends Wisely

"A righteous man is cautious in friendship, but the way of the wicked leads them astray." (Prov. 12:26)

Friendship is something we all need in our lives in order to be healthy and grow into mature individuals. If we isolate ourselves, there is little opportunity to do good, receive good, or to embrace opportunities that stretch us. Scripture warns us to be selective in the area of friendship.

When you think of friend, what do you think of? Many would say a friend is someone with whom you share time, interests, and, often, your life's struggles. It is relaxing to hang out with friends. When I was a teenager, and into my twenties, most of the time that I wasn't in school or at work, I hung out with friends. I found that the attitudes of my friends were contagious. Often their focus became my focus.

When I had any problems, my friends were the ones who helped me through. I didn't go to my parents, my pastor, a counselor, or an expert when I faced difficulties. I went to my friends who were close by, whom I saw almost daily. "The pleasantness of one's friend springs from his earnest counsel" (Prov. 27:9). When we have fed friendships with people of good character, those friends will be more likely to give sound advice. Friends of bad character are more likely to give faulty advice and lead us astray. Friends who base their advice on God's unchanging word will help to keep us on track, making life easier.

Proverbs 22:24–25 says, "Do not make friends with a hot-tempered man, do not associate with one easily angered, or you may learn his ways and get yourself ensnared." As we feed our souls on friendships, our souls are likely to conform to the ways of our friends. If they are partiers, we become partiers. If they are generous, we become generous. If they are angry, we become angry. If they are respectful, we are respectful. If they whine and complain, we whine and complain. It is important to feed good friendships to encourage good fruit. The longer you are around someone, the more likely he will influence you for the good or the bad. You choose your friends, so choose wisely.

Scripture goes so far as to say to avoid foolish people for they will not benefit our lives. It doesn't mean we should be unkind or cruel to people who are foolish, but we should not invest our time and energy in a relationship that would be counterproductive in our lives. "Stay away from a foolish man, for you will not find knowledge on his lips" (Prov. 14:7). We are better off investing our lives in relationships that will bring positive growth, not negative consequences.

Feed friendships that are positive, encouraging, uplifting, inspiring, and that bring you closer to God. Starve friendships that are negative, drag you down, encourage sin, encourage bad habits, or that draw you away from God.

What you feed grows; what you starve dies.

Create Goals

What do you want to achieve in life? Where do you want to be in five, ten, or twenty years? If you want to be married, debt free, have a career, an education, a beach house, a ministry, a network of great friends, close relationships with family, or anything else in life, you must feed that goal. Most goals are not achieved in one fell swoop; they are achieved one small, deliberate step at a time.

God has made us in his image, with desires for relationship, creativity, and enjoying the abundance of his creation. He does not forbid us to plan and dream big dreams. What are your goals? What steps do you need to take to see those goals realized? Don't wait for life to come to you. Go out and follow your dreams. As you move toward your goals, commit them to God. "Commit to the Lord whatever you do, and your plans will succeed" (Prov. 16:3).

Too often we wait for life to open doors for us, so we end up missing opportunities. Scripture encourages us to be proactive. "Ask and it will be given to you; seek and you will find; knock and the door will be opened to you. For everyone who asks receives; he who seeks finds; and to him who knocks, the door will be opened" (Matt. 7:7–8). Asking, seeking, and knocking are all active verbs. They are things God expects and asks of us. We must move beyond the passive attitude that everything will work out, that if it is meant to be it will be. As Christians we know that God will work all things for the good of those who love him, but we are not called to passivity or fatalism.

Take time to examine your life—where it is today, and where you want it to be in five years, ten years and twenty years. If you are married, plan for the future with your spouse. You can also set individual goals. Now decide what actual steps you need to take to accomplish your goals, whether those goals are physical, emotional, or spiritual. Honestly look at your talents and interests. How can you invest and develop these to their full potential? It may mean going to school, paying off debt, changing jobs, moving across the country, becoming more involved at church, volunteering in an organization, or merely practicing an ability.

The old saying is true, "If you aim at nothing, you will hit it every time." So write down your goals and the steps you will take to achieve those goals. Revisit your goals and plans regularly to see how far you have come, and to redirect if necessary. At one point in my life, I thought I wanted to teach English as a second language (TESL). But after taking a few classes, decided I really didn't enjoy that area of study like I thought I would. So I stopped taking TESL classes. Don't be afraid to change course if the one you have chosen isn't working. You may want to add new goals as your life progresses and develops. Feeding your goals and plans today grows a successful abundant future tomorrow.

Think carefully about your goals. Often our society pushes us to make happiness our primary goal. In seeking happiness, we often go about it selfishly—trying to fill our lives with things we enjoy and indulging our sensual nature. Actor Robert Downey Jr. admits that he fell for this lie. His life was a mess, filled with selfishness, drug addiction, and prison. In an interview with Dotson Rader, Downey admits, "I used to be so convinced that happiness was the goal, yet all those years I was chasing after it, I was unhappy in the pursuit. Maybe the goal really should be a life that values honor, duty, good work, friends and family." Happiness truly is a byproduct of a life well lived.

Choosing positive goals for your life also means avoiding what you don't want in your life. Left unattended, most things in life atrophy. This is true in the spiritual, mental, emotional, and physical realms. Be deliberate, proactive, and decisive in the direction of your life. Left unattended, you will drift and float down the broad, easy road that leads nowhere.

What things do you want to avoid in life? Debt, unfaithfulness to your partner, unfaithfulness to God, addictions, evil, broken relationships, bad health, poverty, prison, and getting in a rut? Whatever you don't want in life, you should starve. If any unhealthy things have grown in your life, you can start starving them today. It is often difficult to break those chains. When negative choices have shackled and poisoned us, we may need help from those who have walked the road before us. Don't accept defeat. Help is all around, if you will just ask. See Appendix I for a list of helpful organizations.

What you feed grows; what you starve dies.

18

Balanced Living for the Body, Mind, and Soul

Eat Healthy, Be Healthy; Eat Junk, Be a Chunk

God did not make any two of us exactly alike. Even identical twins have different fingerprints and personalities. Each of our unique bodies differs in the amount of food, rest, and exercise that will enable it to operate optimally. But there are basic guidelines we can all follow for good body performance, which in turn may affect you spiritually.

The old saying "you are what you eat" contains much truth. A steady diet of junk food may not catch up with you for awhile, but eventually it will clog your arteries, put on excess weight and open the door to illness and disease. A diet high in carbohydrates and calories may give you a temporary boost, but is not good for long-term health. Eat for the future. It will arrive sooner than you think!

A variety of healthy foods enables your body to handle the stress of everyday life. We all need protein: meat, poultry, fish, cheese, eggs, seeds, nuts, legumes, and dairy. Essential vitamins, minerals, fiber, and antioxidants are found in abundance in vegetables (darkest colors are best), fruits (darkest colors are best), and whole grains. Water and other fluids are crucial for hydration and flushing the system of toxins. Getting a balance of nutritional foods will help to keep cholesterol low, blood pressure and sugar under control, and ward off cancer and heart disease. While hereditary does affect these things, a healthy diet and healthy weight can often keep potential health problems under control.

Once in a while, most of us eat things that are not good for us—highly processed foods, deep fried, or sugar-filled delights. As long as our basic eating habits are healthy, an occasional splurge should not have a long-term detrimental effect. Jesus was not a legalist when it came to the food we eat. "Don't you see that nothing that enters a man from the outside can make him 'unclean'? For it doesn't go into his heart but into his stomach, and then out of his body. (In saying this, Jesus declared all foods 'clean.')" (Mark 7:18-19).

Be a good steward of the body you have been entrusted. Feed healthy eating habits and reap a healthy body. Feed bad habits and reap sickness and disease. We certainly can accomplish more in our lives if we are healthy than if we are sick. From a purely practical standpoint, it is wise to eat healthy now and reap the benefits now and years down the road.

Get Moving

Along with a healthy diet, a moderate amount of exercise helps to maintain bodily health and wellness. If you are not athletic and have never exercised much, walking is an easy exercise that most people can participate in daily. Even without a gym membership or any home equipment, you can get a cardio workout from a brisk twenty-minute walk. Experts recommend at least twenty minutes, three or four times a week. Benefits of a cardio workout include more energy, reduced stress, increased bone density, better sleep, less anxiety and depression, and a lower risk of heart disease and cancer—a huge return for minimal effort.

Get Your ZZZZZ's

Sleep needs vary from person to person, but most require seven to nine hours to be alert and not sleep deprived. A few need as little as five hours or as much as ten hours. A good night's sleep enhances our memory, learning ability, mood, immune system, and overall health. Don't short your body on sleep. It is the time during which energy is renewed, stress is relieved, and emotions processed. Though you may feel you are getting more done by sleeping less, the opposite is likely true. You are not functioning at your optimum, so your work is not as good, and you may be more irritable and less focused on whatever you are doing. Accidents are also much more frequent when you are tired. So make it a habit to get the sleep you need.

"The U.S. National Highway Traffic Safety Administration estimates that 100,000 of reported crashes occur as a result of drowsiness, and considers sleep deprived drivers a hazard equal in severity to drunk drivers. Studies show that staying awake for 18 hours and driving produces the same effect as being legally drunk behind the wheel. The greater the sleep deprivation, the closer the correlation to higher levels of intoxication."[3]

Spiritual Growth

"Blessed is the man who listens to me, watching daily at my doors, waiting at my doorway. For whoever finds me finds life and receives favor from the Lord." (Prov. 8:34–35)

We grow when we stretch ourselves beyond where we were yesterday. Our growth spiritually is not usually in leaps and bounds, but in small, obedient steps that lead us to greater maturity and Christ-likeness.

Growth starts with knowing the truth. If no action is taken, knowledge is in vain and even counterproductive. Knowledge "puffs up" or may bring pride (1 Cor. 8:1). Applying the truth must follow knowing the truth. Paul tells the Colossians, "We have not stopped praying for you and asking God to fill you with the knowledge of his will through all spiritual wisdom and understanding. And we pray this in order that you may live a life worthy of the Lord and may please him in every way: bearing fruit in every good work, growing in the knowledge of God, being strengthened with all power according to his glorious might" (Col. 1:9–10). Spiritual wisdom and understanding is for the purpose of living a life worthy of God and to produce fruit that allows us to do good works. What does that look like in practical terms?

Teresa has always been a little stingy with her friends, never willing to give of her material blessings. One day Jill came to Teresa, her co-worker and friend with a request. Jill had lost her wallet, which contained her debit card. She asked Teresa for a loan until she could get to the bank. Teresa had a personal policy to never lend money to friends, but she decided to pray about Jill's request. As she prayed, the Holy Spirit brought to her mind the Scripture about "loving your neighbor as yourself." As she thought about Jill's situation, she realized that she would appreciate the loan if she were in the same situation. She knew it wasn't for lack of working or because Jill had squandered her money that she needed a loan; it was because of the accidental loss. Teresa knew she wouldn't be encouraging or supporting a bad habit, but exhibiting Christian love. So she set aside her "personal

---

3. Catie Hayes, "Driving While Tired," http://www.safety.com/articles/driving-while-tired.html.

policy" and lent Jill the money until she could get to the bank. By doing so, she grew. She stretched herself beyond what she normally would have done. She responded to the truth of Scripture and the prompting of the Holy Spirit and became a "doer of the word." The next time someone needed a favor, she would be able to respond with less resistance. Each time Teresa loves her neighbor as herself, it will become more a part of her character and fabric of her being until it is an automatic response. She is being transformed into the image of Christ.

Dave, on the other hand, is very generous by nature. He realizes that he is sometimes too generous, and giving too much may not be the most loving thing to do. George, Dave's neighbor, has borrowed money for rent several times and has never repaid Dave. To continue to pay for George's rent will enable him to continue to squander his money on gambling. George has confided in Dave that he goes to the casinos at every opportunity, and he just can't stop. By continuing to supply rent money, Dave is enabling George to be irresponsible.

Dave's home church group had recently discussed tough love, and he realized that giving without reservation is not the most loving thing he could do for George. So the next time George asked Dave for a rent loan, he gave George the phone number for gamblers anonymous and refused the loan. Dave reasoned that if he had been stuck in the downward spiral George was caught in, that is what he would truly need. Facing his addiction would not be pleasant for George, but it could turn his life around. Dave thought through what it meant to love his neighbor as himself in this situation. It was not a natural thing for him to do, but it was the loving thing, and it has stretched him beyond his natural inclination.

As Christians, we have God's power and strength to draw on as we follow his commands. We don't have to rely on our own ability or capacity. With God's supernatural enabling, we are able to grow beyond our natural ability. We do this out of obedience to Christ and for the purpose of glorifying God. We do this in response to what he has done for us—he became a man, lived a perfect life, died in our place, and lives so that we can have life abundant. He forgives us and extends his grace continually.

Dave and Teresa were both following the command to love their neighbor as they love themselves, though what they did looked different. One obliged a request. The other refused a request. They each had predispositions that led them toward a particular direction, but both were convinced the loving thing was to do the opposite of what they would naturally do. Often there is not a black and white answer in a given situation. It is important to be in a relationship with God, to ask for his leading and guidance in every particular situation. But we should not agonize over the "right" thing. "Do not be anxious about anything, but in everything, by prayer and petition, with thanksgiving, present your requests to God" (Phil. 4:6). We can trust that when we seek God through his word, prayer, and godly counsel, and then follow what we believe is the most biblical way of handling the situation, he will be glorified. "And this is my prayer: that your love may abound more and more in knowledge and depth of insight" (Phil. 1:9).

As we read the word and interact with the world, we should ask for God to open our eyes spiritually, to understand the wisdom of his will and ways, and to have the strength to obey. If we are sincere, God will honor our request and bring glory to his name. It doesn't mean we will never again sin; we will. But when we do, we can go to God, ask forgiveness, make it right with anyone we have wronged, and in the process we will grow spiritually. Following God's ways with God's power makes our lives better than they could ever be on our own. As we respond to God, he blesses us with a better life. This is what it means to have a relationship with Christ. It is truly the ultimate win/win situation!

For more information on the incredible power of the word of God in your life, see Appendix II.

What you feed grows; what you starve dies.

Feeding on TV, Games, Movies, and Books

While we have seen that feeding on the word of God can change who we are, what other things effect our spirit?

Entertainment comes in all kinds of forms. Most are neutral. That is, they don't affect your spiritual life in a positive or negative way unless you are reacting out of a deeper issue. For instance, sports are a great pastime and involve neutral activities. We can gain a lot from sports: teamwork, discipline, skills, good sportsmanship and physical conditioning. Sports can bring incredible enjoyment to those watching or participating. On the other hand, a person who can't lose a game of tennis without throwing a racket across the court is not responding to the sport directly, but to deeper issues of anger and self-image. The sport is intrinsically neutral.

Maya, a young wife, hated sports because her husband, Bob, was always engrossed in a game on TV or was out playing with his friends. Was it really sports she hated? The deeper issue was Bob's failure to nurture his relationship with Maya. When Bob started spending quality time with her and fulfilling his home responsibilities, Maya no longer resented the time he spent engaged in sports. Sports by themselves are not a positive or negative form of entertainment. How we interact with our entertainment is often what causes it to be a positive or negative influence in our lives. We are the determining factor.

Many other pastimes are neutral as well: art, music, TV, movies, books, socializing, dining out, dancing, sightseeing, playing games, boating, hiking, camping, fishing, and most other things with which we occupy our non-working, non-serving, non-sleeping hours. Obviously, some forms of entertainment can be detrimental. We should avoid anything that is illegal or explicitly forbidden in God's word. We should never be involved in: illegal drugs, prostitution, pornography, anything criminal or harming animals or people for entertainment. Feeding on garbage will stink up your life!

But there are some things that fall into more of a gray area. As adults we must decide where we draw the line in the content of movies, games, books, and music lyrics to which we subject ourselves and our children. Scripture is clear that we should fill our minds with things that will not encourage bad behavior or draw us away from God. It is easy to get accustomed to entertainment that promotes the world's view of life. Be very careful that you do not become dull to God's standards by a steady diet of the world's perspective.

The best training for detecting counterfeit money is handling real money, becoming very aware of what it feels and looks like. Then, when a counterfeit bill comes along, we can feel the difference by contrast. Then with closer visual inspection, the counterfeit is found to be "flat," lacking the depth and clarity of a real bill. Likewise, we must have our spirits saturated in God's truth, so that when a lie comes along, we'll recognize it. If we are not careful to know the truth thoroughly, we will more easily buy into a counterfeit way of thinking and behaving.

Hate Evil and Love Good

Both the old and new testaments encourage us to hate evil and love good:

"Hate evil, love good." (Amos 5:15)

"Hate what is evil; cling to what is good." (Rom. 12:9)

Starve Evil

Hating evil entails avoiding it, whether it comes in the form of a person, an activity, an attitude or a thought. "The highway of the upright avoids evil" (Prov. 16:17). Sometimes that is easier said than done.

What do you do if you are working with a person who is arrogant or stirs up dissension? You may not be able to totally avoid her, but you should be careful to stay clear of her influence as much as possible. The closer you get to a person who is involved in things God hates or become involved in them yourself, the messier and more complicated your life will become. Keep your life simple: Avoid evil and evil people.

When I hire an employee, I look closely at the applicant's character. It is not always easy to judge in a half-hour interview, but I have learned the importance of asking insightful questions and calling references. If I know a person has a questionable attitude or character issues, I don't hire him. I have discovered that a bad attitude and poor character of one employee can poison the whole work environment. Skills can be learned if the employee is willing. Attitudes and character are less likely to change in a work environment. I have fired people because they stirred up dissension, stole from the company, or made a habit of lying about their work. One employee I fired for lying burglarized my business that night. He stole essential equipment, so his evil deed set us back for a while. I now wish I had looked more carefully at his character before I hired him.

The evil things God hates or detests fall into two areas. The first area is pride and arrogance. The second is hurting other people. See Appendix III for a list of things God hates. Knowing that involvement in these areas brings great soul toll, we should starve (confess and turn from) them if they surface in our hearts.

Pride was the beginning of the end for the devil and for humanity. Lucifer, the beautiful angel, wanted to be on God's level. When pride entered, his ultimate doom was set. Likewise, when the serpent told Adam and Eve that if they ate from the tree of good and evil they would be like God, they ate. Physical death resulted. Pride is at the root of much evil in the world. Starve any hint of pride you find in your life. Bring it into the light and ask for God's help.

Hurting other people can take many forms—lying, stealing, dishonesty, violence, and murder are found on God's most-hated list. Most would not admit to the above activities, but many of us engage in some form of them occasionally. If you play games or surf the Internet on the computer at work when you are supposed to be working, you are stealing from your employer. He is paying you to work. If you "stretch the truth" to make a sale, you are lying. If you change the statistics on a report to make yourself look better, you are being dishonest. All of these end up hurting others and ultimately ourselves as well. We lose trust, self-esteem and sometimes even a job or a relationship. For your own good, starve things in your life that would hurt others.

Feed Good

Many Bible passages talk about doing good. If we love good, we will do good. Because all of God's commands are good (Neh. 9:13; Rom. 7:12), following his commands is doing good. Jesus proclaimed that all of the commandments fall under two ultimate commands. "Jesus replied: 'Love the Lord your God with all your heart and with all your soul and with all your mind.' This is the first and greatest commandment. And the second is like it: 'Love your neighbor as yourself.' All the Law and the Prophets hang on these two commandments" (Matt. 22:36–40).

If evil consists of various forms of pride and hurting people, the opposite (good) would include humility and helping people. These two concepts follow the two greatest commands. The first command, love God with all we are, will produce humility. While we are fearfully and wonderfully made, we must keep in mind that all we are and have is only because of God. When we love God, we focus on who he is. His magnitude, power, majesty, compassion, and holiness will humble us. The second command, to love our neighbors as ourselves, will naturally result in helping people. Recognizing God has placed us on the earth for "good works" (Eph. 2:10) keeps us serving those in our path. Not only should we do good works, we should be "rich in good deeds" (1 Tim. 6:18). While humility should be a defining attitude, good works should be our hallmark.

We can all do good with our differing gifts and abilities. We should feed our talents and use them for the benefit of others. Linda, a woman with two small children, recently lost her husband. Members of her church group wanted to show their support, so they each "did good" in their own way. For Tara "doing good" was cooking Linda dinner. For Rebecca, the kindest thing she did was not cook Linda's family dinner! But she was able to "do good" by babysitting Linda's children, so Linda could attend to business and take some time for herself. Tony "did good" by helping Linda with yard work. And Jim "did good" by repairing Linda's car. Each one did something different, but all "did good."

We should all "do good" whenever we can, especially helping people in need when they cannot help themselves (and sometimes when they can!). At times doing something nice for a person even if they can do it for themselves is a demonstration of love and support. Everyone needs to know that others are there for them. But we should be aware that it is possible to "do good" and inadvertently enable another to stay irresponsible, addicted, or overly dependent. Pray for God's wisdom as you seek to love your neighbor as yourself. "He has showed you, O man, what is good. And what does the Lord require of you? To act justly and to love mercy and to walk humbly with your God" (Micah 6:8).

19

Slippery Slope

The Innocent Relationship (For Couples and Hopefuls)

Jack and Mary had been married for almost three years when Jack began his "friendship" with Bailey. She was a cute and flirty administrative assistant at his office. Jack enjoyed throwing out jabs and one-liners, so he regularly found himself in "harmless" repartee with Bailey. She obviously enjoyed it and often wandered back to Jack's desk when she wasn't busy up front. He soon realized he looked forward to her short visits. It gave him a break from his hectic pressure-filled day. She looked good, and she was fun. It was nothing serious, just two colleagues having a little fun at a high-stress firm.

Bailey realized Jack responded warmly to her visits, so she managed two or three a day, and on a slow work day would talk for twenty or thirty minutes at a time. She always made sure she touched up her make-up and hair before she went to see him and was thrilled when he started stopping by her desk with pathetic excuses. He would brush her hand lightly with his and pause for just a second or two. He knew she noticed by the way she looked at him. In return, she would touch his arm or shoulder as she talked and enjoyed their flirty dance.

Jack woke up in the morning thinking about Bailey, laughing at their inside jokes. He thought about her when he chose what he would wear for the day. She liked his navy suite, so he wore it often. He also frequently wore the ties she admired, and the cologne she liked was now a regular. When they weren't at each other's desks, they sent e-mails and text messages. Bailey never called or texted Jack at home; she only sent e-mails, not wanting to rouse Mary's suspicion. She knew Jack was "happily" married, but she also was aware of the attention and the "looks" Jack gave her. At home, Jack began to check e-mail much more frequently, and his heart leapt when she sent him a message; he responded immediately, hoping for another contact. If Mary asked who he was e-mailing, he always said it was just work "stuff." The bond between Jack and Bailey was growing stronger. What was happening here?

Jack loved his wife, Mary. They had a good relationship, but Jack had not guarded his heart, as Proverbs 4:23 commands. He opened the door to what he thought was "innocent flirting." What he didn't realize was that he had also opened the door to an affair. He was feeding a fire.

Mary tended to be a worrywart. She was not one to flirt. So the attention Jack received from Bailey brought a new thrill into his life. He began feeling the excitement of a new relationship, and when Bailey engaged his humorous side, his libido surged. Ever so slowly—over months actually—he was deceived into thinking that Mary wasn't enough. That maybe this "innocent" friendship on the side would make up for Mary's worrying personality, as long as he still loved and cared for her. But that didn't happen. His focus and desire gradually shifted from Mary to Bailey.

The Saturday that Bailey, crying and upset, called Jack was a day he had long hoped for. She asked if they could meet somewhere. He felt deep inside that they were destined to be with each other. She made him feel so alive, so appreciated. He had begun to fantasize about what kind of life they could have together. He had rationalized the time and energy he had put into this friendship because it was "a work relationship." It couldn't be cheating. He knew to meet her outside of work would be crossing a line, so he hadn't initiated that. But now she needed him. She was in tears, upset about something, and he could help her, like he did at work when she was overwhelmed. Her phone call and his response began the downward spiral. On his way to meet Bailey, Jack told Mary that he was going to the fitness center to work out. She believed him.

As Jack fed his relationship with Bailey through time, attention, and ultimately physical affection, life became confusing and chaotic. Jack's moral compass was gone. Lies about where he was and what he was doing brought a rift into his relationship with Mary. He became distant and preoccupied. Sin always brings separation. He had cheated on Mary even though he still loved her. His unfaithfulness started with his thoughts and emotions, long before the relationship ever became physical.

As time passed, Jack wanted to be with Bailey more and more until he finally convinced himself that he had never loved Mary, that they were not right for each other from the beginning, and that whatever they did have was gone; they had grown apart over time. He needed to justify his actions to move forward in his relationship with Bailey. So he lied to himself, his friends, his family, and ultimately to Mary as well.

What had Jack fed? His ego, his lust, his pride, his wayward feelings, his thoughts of Bailey, and his attention toward Bailey. What had Jack starved? His humility, his romantic gestures toward Mary, his affection towards Mary, his loyalty and devotion to his wife.

Jack's soul toll for feeding the wrong things was the loss of his marriage, his self-respect, his reputation, and a forced transfer to an office an hour away. The partners at the firm had a strict rule forbidding employees at the same office to date. Soon after he moved in with Bailey, he realized there were things about her he didn't like. She was emotionally unstable, at times blowing up and other times crumbling over small, inconsequential issues. He longed for the stable relationship he'd had with Mary, but it was too late. The trust between them was gone, the divorce was final, and Bailey was pregnant. There was no going back.

Of course, it is not wrong to have friends of the opposite sex, or to joke with them. But male/female relationships are an area where we need to be on guard and perceptive. Sometimes we may not even be aware of another person's attraction to us and gradually we get sucked in or manipulated.

Beware of the following red flags:

Time: A person of the opposite sex is spending a lot of time hanging around, more than they do with anyone else. It could be that they are just lonely. Or it could be trouble. Evaluate if there are other indications that the person is looking for more than a friendship (extended stares, touches, flattery, unmerited gifts or favors, questionable comments, etc.).

Touch: A person of the opposite sex touches you frequently. Some people are just "touchers." If the person hugs and touches everyone, don't worry. If it is just you, be on guard, because the person may have ulterior motives.

Uneasy feeling: If you or your spouse has an uneasy feeling that the person is looking for more in the relationship, beware. Subtle non-verbal cues can indicate more interest than is warranted. These may be processed subconsciously, and we are left with a feeling in the gut that something isn't quite right. Often women pick up on these cues before men do.

Pastor Dr. John Marshall has said that when his wife doesn't feel quite right about the attention a particular woman is showing him, he chooses to avoid the woman as much as possible. He trusts his wife's intuition. Of course, if you are married to a jealous person, you will have to be the judge as to the validity of those feelings. If you cannot speak to someone of the opposite sex without it being a problem for your spouse, there are other issues that need to be dealt with. But for most people, the input of their spouse is valuable in this area. Dr. Marshall could have taken offense at his wife's observations and accused her of not trusting him, but instead he humbly accepted her insight and knew she had his and their best interest at heart.

The following are red flags to address if you see them within yourself:

Excuses: If you find yourself making excuses to see, phone, e-mail, or text the person, beware. Or if you are trying to become friends with his friends, so you can be closer to him, beware. If you are telling yourself "You can't help what you feel," don't listen to that lie. You may not be able to help being attracted, but you can help what you do with those feelings, feeding or starving them.

Attraction: If you are attracted to the person, be on guard that you don't encourage the attraction with time, attention, thoughts, etc. "We take captive every thought to make it obedient to Christ" (2 Cor. 10:5). If you are human, you will be attracted to people. It is not a sin. What you do with your attraction can become sin. Don't feed it, starve it.

Impress: If you find that you are trying to impress the person in how you look, or in what you do or say, beware. If you are frequently volunteering to do favors or help them out when they don't ask, beware (unless you do that with everyone).

Habits: If you find that you are changing your habits because of another person, beware. For instance, your friend loves John Mayer, so you buy his CDs and play them at your desk. Or she has read every Harry Potter book, so you start reading the series, which never appealed to you before. She watches Grey's Anatomy religiously, so you buy the previous seasons you missed to catch up. He is a Red Sox fan, so you become a Red Sox fan. He works out at City Center Fitness, so you start working out there too. You get the idea.

Take Action

If you find that another person is overly interested in you, or you are inappropriately interested in someone else, the best plan is to distance yourself as much as possible. We are to "flee" temptation (1 Cor. 6:18).

Joseph was an excellent example. When temptation came his way, he retreated. "Now Joseph was well-built and handsome, and after a while his master's wife took notice of Joseph and said, 'Come to bed with me!' But he refused. 'With me in charge,' he told her, 'my master does not concern himself with anything in the house; everything he owns he has entrusted to my care. No one is greater in this house than I am. My master has withheld nothing from me except you, because you are his wife. How then could I do such a wicked thing and sin against God?' And though she spoke to Joseph day after day, he refused to go to bed with her or *even be with her* [emphasis mine]. One day he went into the house to attend to his duties, and none of the household servants was inside. She caught him by his cloak and said, 'Come to bed with me!' But he left his cloak in her hand and ran out of the house" (Gen. 39:6–12).

This passage explains that he "refused to even be with her." He didn't entertain the temptation. He didn't toy with it, think about it, or get as close to it as he could without crossing some manmade line. He avoided her. Then when she tried to force herself on him, he "ran out of the house." He physically removed himself. Sometimes that is what it takes to avoid temptation. Joseph paid for his honesty with her false accusations and was thrown into prison. But later God restored him, and he was second in power to Pharaoh. God honored his faithfulness.

You may be a person of great character who would never intentionally seek out an affair, but the affair may seek out you. Never believe that you are above falling. Stay on guard. Don't allow yourself to rationalize or justify an inappropriate relationship. What you feed grows; what you starve dies.

> "It's a slow fade when you give yourself away
> It's a slow fade when black and white have turned to gray
> Thoughts invade, choices are made, a price will be paid
> When you give yourself away
> People never crumble in a day
> It's a slow fade, it's a slow fade"
> (Casting Crowns)

SECTION VI: LIFESTYLE REALITIES

OVERVIEW

Summary

Feeding and starving applies to our growth and health in many areas. We should feed friendships that would influence us for good and starve those that would encourage negative growth. Rather than let life happen to us, we should set goals and take steps to achieve those things, reexamining and adjusting them periodically. We have only one body, so we should take care of it with good nutrition, exercise, and adequate rest. Typically, when we are physically healthy, other areas of our life are also healthier. Spiritual growth comes as we apply God's word to our lives and stretch beyond our natural inclinations. Our choices for entertainment should be thoughtfully reviewed to ensure they do not have a negative influence on us. We should starve evil and feed good in our lives as we humbly serve others. We must be careful to avoid feeding relationships that result in unfaithfulness. We can do this by being aware of red flags in others and ourselves.

Light Reality

- Growth is crucial for an abundant, happy life.
- Positive growth comes from feeding good things and staving bad things.
- We should be proactively engaged in life through positive friendships, goals, healthy lifestyles, and by loving good and hating evil.

Dark Reality

- When we fail to feed the good and starve the bad, we allow things into our life that will bring us harm and destruction.

• Consequences can include poor physical, mental, emotional, and spiritual health.
• Darkness and lack of growth lead to depletion of energy and productivity.
• Deception can lead to a dark reality that brings eventual spiritual death.

Reality Discussion Questions

1. Do your friends encourage you to walk in the light reality or keep you from it? Give an example.

_____

_____

2. What goals have you set for the future?

_____

_____

3. What steps will you take to achieve those goals?

_____

_____

4. How would you rate your diet, exercise, and sleep habits?

_____

_____

5. If necessary, what can you do to improve or change those habits?

_____

_____

6. How would you rate your spiritual habits?

_____

_____

7. If necessary, what can you do to improve or change your spiritual habits?

_____

_____

8. As you read this section, were you prompted to starve anything in your life? If so, what?

_____

_____

9. Retake the quiz at the beginning of Lifestyle Realities. Did you change any of your answers? Which ones and why?

_____

_____

Prayer

Heavenly Father, thank you for the gift of free will. Please help me to make choices that will starve the negative, evil things in my life and feed the good, positive habits and behaviors. Thank you for the gifts and talents you have given me. With your guidance, help me to set goals and take steps to achieve them, so my life is used for your glory. Enable me to choose friends who will be fellow travelers in the light reality. Give me strength to let go of and starve those things in my life that would draw me away from you. In Jesus' name, amen.

SECTION VII: THE DARK REALITY OF LIES

Quiz
Multiple Choice Stories

Choose the *best* answer to the questions below.

1. Lauren and Bobby have dated for about six months and recently started to discuss marriage. They have a lot in common and are committed to each other without reservation. While Bobby always tells Lauren the truth, he often lies to friends, family and coworkers, especially if it gets him out of a jam. He isn't a malicious liar, just a convenient liar. For example, whenever he is late for work, he claims there was an accident or road construction that slowed him down. When called upon to help a friend or family member, he claims he has to work or makes up another excuse. But he doesn't hesitate to ask for help when he is in need. Bobby also lies to elevate himself. On more than one occasion, Lauren has heard him tell her friends stories about his great accomplishments—which she knows are not true. When she confronts him, he says he is just trying to impress her friends.

    "No harm done," he states. "I'm not hurting anyone. Besides, I always tell you the truth. Right, babe?"

    Is Bobby right?

    a. He is partially right; he is not hurting anyone but himself with his lies.

    b. He is right. Lies are neither right nor wrong. No one is hurt by them.

    c. No, he is hurting his relationship with Lauren, those to whom he lies, and himself.

2. Nicole graduated at the top of her class. She majored in sociology and hopes for a future in social work or some other "helping" field. Her work experience before graduation is limited to food service and retail. After graduation, she filled out dozens of job applications and was disappointed when no one called her for an interview. The few local positions in social work were filled, and they will not have any openings in the near future. She has applied for positions in public relations, youth work, and human services. Most require some experience in a related field, but Nicole has none. Desperate for work, she has revised her resume and added some experience at fictitious companies in the town where she went to school. She randomly called numbers until she found some that were no longer in service and listed those as her employment numbers. She hopes that when prospective employers call for a reference at those places, they will assume the companies are out of business. With the added "experience" on her resume, she begins to get calls for interviews.

Should Nicole have embellished her work experience?

    a. Yes. Her "white lies" are not hurting anyone.

    b. No. She has compromised her integrity, and her self-promoting lies could backfire if she is found out.

    c. Yes. Her lies are merely self-protecting. Her degree should be sufficient for success.

    d. No. Her lies are malicious and damaging to others.

    e. a and c above.

TRUE OR FALSE?

The Dark Reality of Lies

True/False 1. All lies are the same and have the same consequences.

True/False 2. It is okay to lie if you are protecting someone's feelings.

True/False 3. When it comes to emotions, you can't help what you feel.

True/False 4. Denial is a healthy defense mechanism to cope with difficult situations.

True/False 5. When we ignore problems, they usually just resolve on their own.

True/False 6. Lies hurt only the person telling them.

True/False 7. It is possible to be too honest; we should not always express what we are thinking.

True/False 8. When trust is lost in a relationship and the offending person repents, the hurt party should begin to trust the offender immediately.

True/False 9. A person who is sorry about hurting someone else is repentant.

True/False 10. If we walk in the light, we will never stumble or fall.

20

Types of Lies

"Rather, we have renounced secret and shameful ways; we do not use deception, nor do we distort the word of God. On the contrary, by setting forth the truth plainly we commend ourselves to every man's conscience in the sight of God." (2 Cor. 4:2)

Our society is experiencing a deluge of lies. From presidents down to the common man, it is no longer considered wrong to lie. In fact, it is expected. We hear characters lying in almost every movie or fictional show. See how long it takes to find a movie or series in which no one lies. In the TV drama, "House," Dr. House frequently proclaims, "Everyone lies." Unfortunately, our entertainment reflects the reality of American society today. It was not so fifty years ago. It is a sad commentary about the direction our nation is heading.

Intentional and Unintentional Lies

Lies bring darkness and deception, whether they are intentional or unintentional. At one time or another, we have all deliberately changed the truth or not told the entire truth. Intentional lies should make us feel some sorrow. We have violated our conscience and discarded reality. If lying doesn't cause some twinge of "I shouldn't have said that," we need to examine our hearts. Are we distorting the truth so often that we've hardened our spirits and souls against the work of conscience and the Holy Spirit?

Often, deliberate lies can become fuzzy, and we can confuse them with the truth if we tell them frequently enough. Have you ever caught someone in a lie that you initially believed because they were so convincing? He rehearsed the lie so often that he convinced himself it was true. These are dangerous lies that pull a person into the dark realm of self-deception.

What should we do when we admit to ourselves that we have lied? The next step is to set the record straight and repair any damaged relationships. We should also confess our failure to God and ask for his help to turn from lying. God is able to change our hearts. Do not underestimate the seriousness of this habit. A devouring lie perpetuated by our culture is that lying is no big deal. Unfortunately, a habit of lying seems only to worsen over time, for lies perpetuate lies.

Unintentional lies are of less consequence to our souls, but often bring crazy results into our lives. God judges us based on our heart, so if we are unaware that we are propagating a lie by our behavior, he extends more grace and mercy until his truth breaks through. For example, if we believe that we are showing God's love by supporting an alcoholic cousin who is unwilling to work, then we will reap a world of chaos and enablement. God will eventually bring us around to understand that true love would not enable an addict, but would help him to get treatment and to learn to take responsibility for his own life.

When we understand the truth, we are responsible to act on it and stop enabling poor, weak cousin Joe. All of us have propagated unintentional lies by living in alignment with false assumptions. Such living can hurt us, as well as others around us. As we study God's word and stay open to the Holy Spirit, we will recognize these unintentional lies and move into truth and learn to walk on the light path. Life will become less crazy and chaotic when we live in reality.

Christians have fallen for a number of lies that are not supported by scripture. For example, John, a young father, believes that Christians shouldn't become angry (a false perception). So he acts on that understanding. His supervisor is abusive; he constantly ridicules John and keeps him late every night. John tells himself that he can't become angry, so he holds his feelings in and starts to develop an ulcer. His relationships suffer because he isn't home very much, and when he is home, he is tired and stressed, so he lashes out at his family. One false assumption has infiltrated John's entire life. His work and home life are deteriorating because he is holding onto and acting on a false premise, a lie.

The truth, on the other hand, would have brought about a different scenario. When John's supervisor mistreated him, it would have caused anger, which when handled correctly could bring about positive change.

He wouldn't have felt guilt for his anger; he would understand it is a God-given emotion to signal that there is a problem that needs attention (either internal or external). He could have approached his boss, confronted him with the injustice and tried to resolve the issues in a healthy manner. Either the situation would have been resolved (if the supervisor responded positively) or John's supervisor could have continued to be unfair. Then John would have to decide if he was going to accept that unfair behavior or find another job. Either way, he would have faced his anger, directed it toward solving the problem positively and improved the situation.

John's inaccurate belief was something he had grown up with and heard from the pulpit. "Anger is a sin. If you are a Christian you should not become angry." But that is not what Scripture says. It says, "Do not let the sun go down while you are still angry" (Ephes. 4:26). It assumes that you will be angry. Anger is a healthy, motivating emotion. On the other hand, you can't assume that every time you are angry you are right to be upset. But your angry feeling is not a sin until you mismanage it. It is a signal that something is wrong. It is an opportunity to examine your heart, try to understand what your motive is in the anger—whether justified or unjustified—and, if justified, what positive resolving action should follow. (See Gary Chapman's book *Anger: Handling a Powerful Emotion in a Healthy Way* for a balanced understanding of anger.)

False perceptions remain until we embrace the truth. Inaccurate beliefs can be altered by consuming a healthy diet of Scripture, following the leading of the Holy Spirit, listening to teaching from a good Bible-based church, and fellowshipping with other believers. We are also influenced by our entertainment diet, so we need to make sure that we are not taking in a steady diet of lies.

Motive

Why would a person deliberately throw out truth in favor of a lie? Embrace darkness instead of light? Choose to live in unreality? The reasons are endless and sometimes complex.

We might embrace lies for self-protection, or to save face or avoid consequences for poor behavior. Sometimes people are egotistical or insecure and tell self-promoting lies to pretend they are something they are not. Still others are jealous, competitive, or revengeful and tell lies that damage others. The reasons for telling lies that damage other people are numerous. Such lies are the most serious types of lie. In contrast, another common reason for telling a lie—usually called a "white lie"—is to save someone from being hurt or damaged in some way. Other lies, such as denial or lying to yourself, are defense mechanisms. The truth is just too painful or difficult to deal with, so we lie to ourselves. People lie for many different reasons.

Protecting Lies

Some of the most common lies are those that protect us from getting into trouble. No one wants to have their boss mad at them, but Melissa learned her lesson the hard way. She and her coworker Karen were putting shelves up at their retail store. Melissa's boss had previously seen them both on the ladder and warned them that it was against store safety policies. But when a shelf started to slip out of Karen's hands, Melissa climbed onto the ladder with Karen to help. Karen lost her balance and tumbled down on top of Melissa. Karen ended up with a chipped tooth and needed stitches in her lip. Melissa had a cut knee and some bruises. The manager asked them to tell her what happened. Because they feared reprisal, they insisted that Melissa was standing beside the ladder when the accident happened.

The manager then told them that an assistant manager had seen Karen and Melissa on the ladder together. Karen was demoted from her department manager's position for breaking policy and then lying about it. If she had told the truth—that Melissa was on the ladder and the shelf she was installing started slipping, so Karen climbed the ladder to help her—she may have been able to keep her position. Instead of protecting her, the lie hurt her.

Lying to protect ourselves is a natural reaction, but it does not build our character or connection to the truth and reality. We are much better off to just tell the truth—even if it hurts or we are rejected. We will be respected for owning up to our mistakes, bad choices, and poor judgments. We may suffer consequences, but often they will be less severe than if we lie and are caught doing so. Even if we are not caught lying, we won't retain our self-respect or have a clear conscience with God and man. When our conscience is not clear, we have to lie to ourselves to convince ourselves we did the right thing. Lies can become more convoluted the longer we hang on to them. We have to justify and rationalize our lies. Life is simpler when we just tell the truth. "So I strive always to keep my conscience clear before God and man" (Acts 24:16).

Self-promoting Lies

Have you ever met someone who needs the approval of others so badly that she will lie about everything in order to be accepted? She is insecure in the reality of who she is, so she becomes someone else. While running a Christian dating service, I talked to numerous individuals who had tried secular services and encountered self-promoting liars. People who claimed to be single, but were married; people who claimed to be wealthy, but were struggling financially; people who claimed to have a great education or occupation, but had neither. They were not what they were presenting themselves to be. The person the client thought she was dating didn't exist. He was an imaginary image built on self-promoting lies.

What would motivate people to say they are someone else? It is most likely the insecurity of acknowledging who they really are. They are not happy with reality, so they present another persona. If that person is rejected, at least the person isn't really rejecting them, for that persona is not who they truly are. Or they may have issues of pride. They feel entitled to be honored and esteemed. They think they are better than they actually are, so they make lies to receive the treatment they believe they deserve. Either way, they cannot have a genuine relationship because they are not being honest about themselves. So their relationships are shallow and unfulfilling until they learn to find acceptance in God's unconditional love and to be authentic with those around them.

Lies that Damage Others

The most devastating lies are those that bring harm to others. Lies born out of hurtful motives are lies that God hates the most. Why do people tell lies about others? The reasons are twofold. Some lie out of selfishness. Others lie for the sole purpose of hurting another person.

People have many different motives for selfish lies:

- Jealousy
- Attention
- The love of chaos
- Insecurity—trying to create more self-value by putting another down
- Avoidance of trouble—by blaming someone else for their poor behavior
- Competitiveness—knocking another person out of the game

All of these motives are self-serving, but in the end they hurt others and do not please God. People who tell these lies may not even realize they are hurting others because they are so focused on themselves and the end product that they want to achieve.

On the other hand, some people lie fully intending to hurt others:

- They are cruel or mean-spirited.
- They have sadistic desires and gain perverse pleasure when they hurt people.
- They want revenge.
- They want to control and abuse.
- They want power.
- They want to manipulate others.

Whenever we lie about those who are innocent, we set ourselves in opposition to God. He is truth. He is for people. He loves the light and the right. If we, God's children, tell lies that hurt others, he will discipline us in some way; we can count on it. God, the ultimate parent, wants us to grow in his ways of kindness and encouraging others, not in tearing them down. Somehow, he will get our attention, so that we can repent and make it right. If you realize you have erred in this way, ask him to show you the best way to make the situation right. He is gracious and will forgive and can turn around broken relationships.

"White Lies"

While a "white lie" is still wrong, God judges us by the motive of our heart. A lie told to damage someone is a much greater offense than a lie told to keep someone from being hurt. It is best to speak the truth in love, which is often harder than telling a "white lie" because the truth may not be well-received—even when told in love. We may face anger or rejection. Resist telling "white lies." Loving the truth brings better results in our life. It keeps life simple and real.

Katie was dating a great man, Jeff. They had told each other all about their lives and significant history. But Katie kept one small secret from Dan so she wouldn't hurt him. She had been engaged to his roommate before he was Jeff's roommate. When she started dating him, she didn't know he was rooming with Ryan, her ex-fiancé. She felt it could damage their relationship if he knew they had been engaged. So she asked Ryan not to tell Jeff. She reasoned that it really wasn't a lie, just an omission or maybe a white lie. But, Ryan let the truth slip one day, and her deception nearly destroyed her relationship with Jeff. Instead of protecting him from being hurt, she caused more hurt by her lie. The truth may have been difficult initially, but would have, in the long run, been less painful than the deception.

Denial (Lying to Ourselves)

If we are prone to this defense mechanism of denial, we may not even realize what is taking place. These lies can have the greatest grip on us. In order to let go of them, we must be willing to experience the pain that accompanies truth. It is important to examine our hearts before God regularly to ensure we are not living in denial. Life won't get better until we confront the truth and live in reality.

Hard truth comes to all at one time or another. How we deal with challenging truths today will make life easier or harder in the long run. Some say to acknowledge difficulty and suffering is the first step to transcending it. Obviously, acknowledgement is the first step in dealing with it, but, if we are honest, we don't transcend problems by merely acknowledging difficulty as a human common denominator. Yes, it will help us to avoid the "poor me" syndrome, and it will help us to put our trials into perspective, but it will not make them unimportant or insignificant.

Problems are, in fact, one layer of our life on earth—an unpleasant layer, but a very real, very important layer. Those who deny this layer live in a false reality with which they will one day crash head-on. But until that happens, they choose to ignore the issues in front of them, acting as if problems will resolve on their own. Left unattended, most problems become worse or more complicated, rather than diminished or simplified.

As a young married woman of twenty-four, Jill came face to face with the reality of child abuse. The wonderful, charming man she had married was a Dr. Jekyll/Mr. Hyde personality. He could be delightfully witty and intelligent one moment, and deteriorate into a raving, violent, irrational perpetrator the next. Because of her rigid religious beliefs, she chose to deny and compartmentalize, not really dealing with the issue for many years. Much to her dismay, the problem did not naturally go away, but became much worse over time. Problems need to be addressed directly, honestly, and swiftly, so the natural decay and complication has no time to set in. The longer a problem is left to germinate in unreality, the worse it gets.

Jill was thirty-four when she finally took decisive action concerning her husband's abuse. By then she had suffered years of emotional turmoil and guilt, and had little self-esteem. Her children likewise had suffered emotionally and physically. Her husband had been enabled to continue the abuse, which had become the family's norm, and he had no motivation to stop. Denial, ignoring or pretending issues don't exist are defense mechanisms that work only temporarily. Truth ultimately breaks through.

The reality is that Jill was living with a child abuser. He was physically and emotionally abusive. She didn't want to face the reality, but she was aware of it on a subconscious level. She categorized the abuse as a shortcoming, a weakness, or a typical male anger issue. Rationalizing the abuse enabled her to at least acknowledge, but minimize the issue. The denial was partial, but enough of an anesthesia that she didn't face it head on until her eight-year-old daughter started talking about suicide because of the abuse. She was married to a child abuser; she had to face that reality.

Lies often grow. One little lie becomes two, which then becomes three, and eventually an ever-growing monster that we shouldn't allow into our lives. The consequences of lies (deliberate, self-protecting, self-promoting, damaging, "white lies," and denial) are detrimental to our relationships and growth as individuals. We are unable to move forward or deeper because we do not love the truth. "They perish because they refused to love the truth and so be saved" (2 Thess. 2:10).

21

Lies Cost

Consequences of Lies

Living in unreality—Lies distort our reality. We project false stories and images to others and often end up believing them. When we live out of sync with the truth, we live in a world that doesn't exist. We try to avoid the principles that God set in place, but end up crashing headlong into them. God's eternal principles stand firm. Any lie stands in opposition to his truth. We will eventually pay soul toll if we live a life of lies, for lies place us on the dark path and create hardness in our souls. The spiritual blindness is gradual as light fades away and reality can no longer be perceived. Lies replace truth. Darkness replaces light. They cannot coexist.

Confusion—Lies keep the truth at bay, so life doesn't make complete sense. The truth brings clarity and answers questions. Lies only muddy the water. The more lies, the murkier the water. When you look into cloudy water, you can't see what is in it. You can only guess and hope nothing dangerous awaits you. If you want to see clearly and live in the truth, you must forsake lies. Truth is not always pretty, but it is clear. Don't settle for a confusing, muddy reality. It won't keep your spirit on track and bring you the peace that comes from walking in the light. Seek after God, and you will find the truth, for he is truth. He promises to be found when you seek him, and he will give you grace to deal with any difficult truth.

Joel decided to lie about his whereabouts to his boss, Mike. He had a second job, and that was prohibited by his contract. He told Mike that his wife, Marilyn, was sick, and he needed to take her to the doctor. But the truth was that he'd had to work overtime to finish a project with a strict deadline at his other job. After Joel used his "sick wife" excuse three or four times for missing work, Mike told his wife, Carrie, that Marilyn was quite sick. Joel and Mike's wives happened to be friends and neighbors. Carrie bought a card and some flowers and showed up at Marilyn's door. Of course, Marilyn told her friend she wasn't sick (she had no idea her husband had been lying), and things quickly became complicated—ending with a reprimand and a forced decision. Joel had to decide between his two jobs.

Joel had created confusion, left his coworkers short staffed, broke the trust he had with Mike and with Marilyn, and even damaged Marilyn's relationship with her friend Carrie. Lying led to more lying. The first lie was taking the forbidden second job—he had signed a contract saying he would not do so. He covered that lie with more lies. As is often the case, one lie led to another. Don't start down that road. It does not end well.

Heartache—A lifelong habit of lying will backfire and bring you trouble. Since lies are out of step with reality, they will eventually surface for what they are and cause heartache, as they did with Joel. Those affected by them, either directly or indirectly, including the liar will be hurt. A lie may be expedient, but in the end it will bite. How much better to feel a little pain initially by telling the truth, than suffer the far-reaching consequences of lies that have multiplied into a boatload of pain, affecting many. "A deceitful tongue crushes the spirit" (Prov. 15:4). You will be held accountable for the ripple effect of your lies.

What could Joel have done differently to avoid heartache in the above story? He could have told Mike he wasn't making ends meet on his current salary. He could have asked about extra projects or possible promotions or raises that might be available. If none were available, he could have requested permission to hold a part-time job with a company that wasn't a competitor to his employer. Other options were available. He didn't have to lie. The heartache (or soul toll) would have been much less. As it was, his deceit damaged his own reputation and character, hurt his coworkers, caused a loss of trust with his boss and his wife, and hurt the relationship between Carrie and Marilyn. The ripple effect of lies is real.

Superficial relationships—When relationships lack trust, which comes from truth, they will remain superficial. Lies, betrayals, and truth withheld can stop the progress of growing deeper in understanding and closeness. Once lies enter into a dynamic, the bridge of trust is lost, and a wall of mistrust is set up. All future interactions are filtered through mistrust. Only through confession and time will the relationship be able to move forward. As long as there is no confession or repentance, there will be no progress toward a deeper relationship. True repentance will be proved over time, or it will be shown to be false. If no true repentance is exhibited, the relationship will stagnate or deteriorate. Relationships can only be built on and grow through truth and love.

Wrong family—When you live a life of lies, you are aligning yourself with the wrong family. God's children should walk in the light and truth. You cannot align yourself with the families of light and darkness at the same time. Jesus was clear; a house divided against itself cannot stand. You must choose whether your life will be one of truth or lies. And you must know that when you choose lies, you choose Satan. Jesus spoke clearly to the Jews who wanted to kill him, "You belong to your father, the devil, and you want to carry out your father's desire. He was a murderer from the beginning, not holding to the truth, for there is no truth in him. When he lies, he speaks his native language, for he is a liar and the father of lies" (John 8:44). Don't settle for Satan's family; they do not have your best interest at heart. God and his family do.

22

Truth Pays

"For you were once darkness, but now you are light in the Lord. Live as children of light (for the fruit of the light consists in all goodness, righteousness and truth)." (Eph. 5:8–9)

Remedy for Lies—Truth/Honesty

While walking in the light, we may stumble and fall, but we will be able to see to get back up. No one is without fault or sin. Fortunately, God's grace extends to our poor choices, blatant sins, and ignorant mistakes. If we confess and repent, he promises to restore our relationship with him. If you don't hunger for love or truth, tell God about it and ask him to transform your heart. He knows anyway and will bring those changes into your life, if you are willing.

Repentance can also help to restore the relationships we have damaged with lies, but he does not guarantee that will happen. He cannot force another person's reaction to your repentance. They may receive you with open arms, or they may choose not to forgive and the relationship may remain broken.

Embracing truth leads us down a path of honesty in our personal and professional lives. And honesty is foundational to integrity. Without honesty, we have no integrity. The more honest we become, the more light shines on our path. And where light is, darkness cannot abide. But the more lies we entertain, the darker our path becomes.

The truth is stronger than lies. Lies have no substance, no reality, and no power. A life full of lies has no substance, no reality, and no power. The truth is bold, solid, and powerful. A person of truth is bold, solid, and powerful. I recently saw an interview with two people who were running for a political office. The liberal candidate did not want to answer the questions truthfully because he knew he would lose any potential voters in that conservative audience. So he hedged and fudged and generalized. He gave many non-answers, sidestepping what he really thought. His evasion made him appear weak. His lies diluted his reality—who he really was and what he really stood for.

His opponent, on the other hand, answered boldly, decisively, and directly. He came across as a person who was solid and powerful. The candidate who was indirect and circumvented the truth hurt himself because he came across as wishy-washy. If he had answered honestly, he would have retained the respect of many for standing by his beliefs, but he lost respect when he tried to dishonestly please his audience.

Unnecessary "Truthfulness"

Does that sound like an oxymoron? In college, I had two good friends who decided that they would be completely honest with each other, regardless of the consequences or of the feelings of the other. While honesty is always the best policy, blurting out everything we think is not wise or beneficial. My two friends began to tell each other when they felt the other one wore something ugly, or made them look fat, or that their hair was particularly frizzy that day. They criticized each other mercilessly. In essence, they became petty and catty—on the verge of ruining a good friendship. The atmosphere around them became tense and both came to resent the other's "honesty." A quest for truth and honesty ended in relational disaster. It was not motivated by love, but by a warped understanding of truth.

God has given us thoughts and words. They are not to be confused. We can direct thoughts, though we cannot completely control the first thing that comes to mind. God has also given us words for which we are accountable. He expects us to choose our words wisely. We are not instructed to speak every thought that goes through our minds—especially when we would needlessly hurt or damage another person. It shows a lack of discernment and control when every word we think must be spoken. That is not honesty and truth; it is an elevation of our thoughts to God's truth. It is never so.

Our thoughts should be subject only to God's view, and I often find myself examining and repenting of thoughts that I know are in opposition to God's love and mercy. Thankfully, he has given us a buffer between our thoughts and words. May we take full advantage of this chasm and use our words intentionally for good and not evil.

SECTION VII: THE DARK REALITY OF LIES

OVERVIEW

Summary

Society has accepted lying as normal and expected, minimizing its real effects. Lying creates a false reality and havoc in your world. Intentional and unintentional lies bring chaos, but intentional lies also harden your soul. Lies fall into several categories—self-protecting, self-promoting, lies that damage others, white lies and self-deceiving lies. The consequences of lies are living in unreality, darkness, confusion, heartache, superficial relationships, and alignment with the wrong powers. To find clarity and power, we should pursue a life of honesty and truth found only in God.

Light Reality

- God is truth. To live a life of genuineness, we must commit to honesty and truth, even when it hurts.
- We should avoid causing needless hurt to others by poorly motivated "truthfulness."
- Truth brings power to transform and strengthen our character.

Dark Reality

- Lies bring pain, lack of trust, confusion, heartache, and darkness.
- Dishonesty obliterates the truth and light, and brings stagnation to our souls.
- When we engage in lies, we are entering Satan's territory. He will keep us in darkness if we live a life of lies. Don't give him that pleasure.

Reality Discussion Questions

1. How often do you lie or tell a half truth?

_____

_____

2. What is your usual motivation?

_____

_____

3. Tell about a time a lie hurt one of your relationships

_____

_____

4. When has one lie led to another lie?

_____

_____

5. When have you told a selfish lie that hurt others?

_____

_____

6. When have you told a lie to deliberately hurt another?

_____

_____

7. When did someone tell a lie that hurt you?

_____

_____

8. When have you chosen to tell the truth, even though it hurt?

_____

_____

9. Retake the quiz at the beginning of The Dark Reality of Lies. Did you change any of your answers? Which ones and why?

_____

_____

Prayer

Heavenly Father, please help me to be aware of different types of lies that exist in my life. Help me to reject denial in any form and be willing to live my life in truth and the light of your spirit. If I have hurt others with lies, please forgive me and give me the courage to make things right. Thank you for your grace, which covers over all my sins when I repent. Keep me on a path of light and truth. In Jesus' name, amen.

SECTION VIII: SPIRITUAL REALITY

Quiz

Multiple Choice Stories

Choose the *best* answer to the questions below.

1. Jake has had a rough life. His father abandoned him, his mother, and two younger sisters when he was nine. Distraught, his mom became an alcoholic, unable to keep a job or care for her family. Jake ended up parenting his sisters. They scraped by, only surviving with government assistance. When Jake was sixteen, he got a job at a car dealership to supplement the family's meager income. He had a good relationship with his boss and over several years worked his way into management. Jake supported his sisters until they moved out on their own. And now, at twenty-three years old, he continues to support his mother, so she won't end up on the street. But bitterness toward her has crept in; consequently, he never visits or calls. Jake believes he is a righteous person because he supported his sisters and continues to support his mother, in spite of his bitterness. He believes he doesn't need God; he is a self-made man.

What is wrong with Jake's thinking?

   a. There is nothing wrong with Jake's thinking. He is a righteous man. He has made the most of what life has dealt him. His mother and father both let him down, but he picked up the slack for his sisters' benefit. He has a right to be bitter. Jake should be proud of his accomplishments.

   b. Jake does not recognize that God gave him his abilities to work and earn income to be able to support his family.

He needs God's help with the bitterness he has allowed in his heart.

c. If Jake restores the relationship with his mother, then he would be a righteous man. It is best to live at peace with everyone.

d. None of us are righteous in God's eyes. We all need forgiveness and spiritual healing. These only come through Jesus' death on the cross in our place.

e. b and d

2. Gabby grew up in a family of givers. From her great grandmother down, all of the family has been involved in charities and worthy projects. The latest is a fundraiser for the victims of Haiti's great earthquake. Gabby has set up an internet site and is funneling money for food, clothes, and medical supplies for the thousands living in tent cities. Gabby's position in the local chamber gives her a large network of businesses to solicit in times of need. Everyone loves Gabby; she is truly a selfless person. She considers herself spiritual, though she doesn't follow rituals or religious traditions of any church. She meditates daily and visualizes good things for herself, her family, her community, and the world. She has a sense of purpose and a strong drive to achieve great things in her life. She feels a oneness with nature and the universe.

Is Abby living in spiritual reality?

a. Yes, she has tapped into the great collective consciousness of all humanity.

b. Yes, she has found a spiritual path of good works handed down from her family. She looks within to find peace in her soul. All religions and spiritual paths are ultimately the same.

c. No, she is missing the supremacy of God in the universe and her relationship to him as a created being in need of his reconciling work through Jesus.

d.   No, she is not doing enough to please God. She doesn't attend church, pay tithes, or follow religious traditions.

3.   Joe is the owner of an extremely successful parasailing business in a southern coastal tourist town. He spends May through October on the water and has the luxury of closing his business over the winter. He spends off season enjoying his hobbies, family and friends. Joe attends church every Sunday, and reads his Bible and prays most days. But whenever Joe is asked to contribute either financially or with his time and energy, he declines. He reasons that he has worked hard all summer, seven days a week, to supply for his family. The winter is *his* time—to refresh and relax. And because his work is seasonal, Joe deliberately conserves his money in case a slow season is ahead. But he will occasionally drop a $10 or $20 bill in the offering.

Joe's thinking is _____.

a.   accurate. He is doing his part in supplying for his family. That is all God asks of him.

b.   partially accurate. He isn't obligated to give his time and energy beyond working to supply for his family, but he should contribute more financially since his business is doing so well.

c.   inaccurate. All he has is God's, and he is just a manager. While he needs to take care of himself and his family, he should also be open to give of his time, money and energy to others during the off season.

d.   inaccurate. He is just being lazy and should get another job during the winter months, so he will have more for his family if business slows down. The economy isn't what it used to be.

TRUE OR FALSE?

Spiritual Reality

True/False 1. As long as you follow your heart, you will be on track spiritually.

True/False 2. Physical laws are not the ultimate laws of the universe.

True/False 3. The suffering in the world shows that God doesn't really care about people.

True/False 4. When life is unfair, we are justified to complain.

True/False 5. Our focus in life should be on self-actualization and fulfillment.

True/False 6. True spirituality is found within ourselves.

True/False 7. The secret to getting what we want out of life is visualizing it.

True/False 8. We are only accountable to ourselves for what we do with our time, talent, and possessions.

True/False 9. It is okay to believe whatever we want as long as we are consistent in living what we believe.

True/False 10. What will be will be; our choices won't change what has been predetermined.

23

Trust the Alternate Reality

"So we fix our eyes not on what is seen,
but on what is unseen. For what is seen is temporary,
but what is unseen is eternal." (2 Cor. 4:18)

What Is Real?

Everyone thinks they have a handle on reality—the way things really are. Just listen to talk radio. You'll hear it all. Someone will tell you how to vote, what to believe, what to buy, how to handle your money and investments, and even how to handle your children and in-laws. We all have an opinion. While it is important to glean as much truth from others as possible, we must ultimately let God's word, the ultimate truth, guide us.

While visiting my son and daughter-in-law, we took some family photos. I had accidentally left the camera setting for outdoor lighting, because I had been taking pictures at the beach. Consequently, the lens let in less light than was needed indoors, and the first candid shots were dark, and the color was way off. By the time we took the posed family shots, my husband had discovered my mistake and made the needed adjustments. The posed photos turned out beautifully. I tried to doctor the candid shots, but couldn't get them to match reality.

Such is our life when the settings of our soul are out of sync with truth. We operate on a basis that is not in alignment with reality, and we see life distorted and out of focus. Consequently, we behave in ways that are not in our best interest because we are not seeing truth clearly.

Saul's Reality

An excellent example of following a false reality exists in the life of Saul, also called Paul. He was following what he thought was God's will and plan for his life. Saul was a Jew born in Tarsus of Cilicia, but brought up in Jerusalem. He was trained under Gamaliel in the religious laws. A Pharisee, he was zealous for God, persecuting followers of Jesus by throwing them into prison and having them killed. His reality was that Jesus was a false prophet and people who followed him were blaspheming the true God. Saul himself says God was merciful because he acted in ignorance and unbelief. Saul realized his previous understanding of reality was not true. He was acting and reacting to what he believed was reality.

God intervened in a supernatural way on the road to Damascus, so Saul could exchange his false beliefs for truth:

> "As he neared Damascus on his journey, suddenly a light from heaven flashed around him. He fell to the ground and heard a voice say to him, 'Saul, Saul, why do you persecute me?'
> 'Who are you, Lord?' Saul asked.
> 'I am Jesus, whom you are persecuting,' he replied. 'Now get up and go into the city, and you will be told what you must do.' (Acts 9:3–6)

Paul's religious beliefs were entrenched in the false reality that led him to persecute the church, thinking he was serving God. Fortunately, God's grace and mercy extend to all of us in our ignorance and unbelief. If God can forgive and redirect Paul, who murdered believers, God can forgive and redirect each of our lives when our reality is not real!

The following contrast some of the world's misconceptions with actual spiritual reality.

World's Reality: The visible is most real.

Spiritual Reality: The unseen is most real.

Focusing on the physical is easy. We see, hear, touch, taste, and smell hundreds of things daily. Our senses are bombarded by electronic media: TVs, radios, iPod's, iPhones, video games, cell phones, podcasts, iTunes, and computers. In addition to all that noise, we face daily traffic, work activity, civic or church activity, hobbies, and friends and family. With so much distraction, it is no wonder we often ignore the unseen, the spiritual, the absolute reality.

Beyond space and time, God exists. He always was, always is, and always will be. Nothing and no one compares to Him. His human creatures are body, soul, and spirit. And God has ordained laws to govern each of these realms. When we learn the laws that affect our lives and abide by them, life becomes easier and more harmonious because we are staying within the governing limits of that realm.

Physical Laws

Every individual has to come to terms with physical laws in his or her body. We must have some sleep, some food, some exercise, and some care for our body. If these things are not attended to, bad things happen. A sleep-deprived person eventually will go insane. Food and water deprivation lead to sickness and death. A profound lack of exercise leads to weakness and illness. And lack of hygiene can lead to bad smell, sickness, decay, and rotting teeth. People act on the reality of physical laws every day without even thinking about them.

Many professions base their work on physical laws. Doctors treat patients with drugs that affect their bodies in a particular way. Scientists create new forms of energy based on physical research. NASA sends men into space and conducts research based on physical laws. Engineers, architects, and home builders all depend on these laws to do their work. Physical laws are real, and few try to deny that they exist.

Defying physical laws can be disastrous. A little boy wants to fly, so he climbs onto the roof, jumps off, and crashes into the ground below. Physical laws keep him from flying, floating, or landing softly. We have all learned about certain physical laws in school: gravity, centrifugal force, centripetal force, boiling point, freezing point. We accept that our universe is set to work in a certain way based on certain principles. They may seem arbitrary to us, but we know they exist.

Believing or wishing physical laws were different, doesn't change them. The same is true with soul and spiritual laws, even though we don't always see the results with our eyes when they are broken.

Soul Laws

Soul laws are very real and quite predictable. Soul laws can be defined as the principles that govern psychological behavior. If given information about a person's behavior, profilers can make inferences about the psychological make-up that will govern other aspects of that person's conduct. These laws allow fairly accurate predictions about individual future actions.

The last two decades have seen a rash of TV crime shows, many of which revolve around soul laws. *Profiler, Law and Order: Criminal Intent,* and *Criminal Minds* are particularly adept at identifying soul laws. Each show portrays characters who solve crimes based on soul laws. A profile of the type of person who would commit the crime is accurately presented long before the actual culprit is caught. Motives are deduced based on circumstances, and the guilty party is apprehended.

Such shows are based on profilers who have studied soul laws in relationship to crime. Students of human behavior can "profile" certain types of criminals based on soul laws and narrow the search for the "unsub" (the unknown subject). Soul laws reveal the unseen truths and predict future actions of the criminal that result in capture. Of course, physical evidence to support the profiler's theory is helpful for conviction. It is easier to convict a person based on concrete evidence, rather than on conclusions about motive or psychological patterns.

Because soul laws cannot be seen, we usually trust them less, though they are very real. Psychiatrists and psychologists spend their lives studying soul laws and dedicate their careers to helping people to understand and follow soul principles that will make their lives better. Most people accept as true simple soul laws such as "holding a grudge will damage the person holding it," or "a positive attitude will encourage a positive outcome."

More complex soul dynamics occur in many situations which, when understood, give insight for creating better relationships. For example, victims in abusive situations are often of a certain personality type. They are typically compliant, nurturing, co-dependent, or people-pleasing individuals. Abusers are able to continue to perpetrate because of the personality characteristics of those they are abusing. Soul principles dictate that the longer compliant people are in abusive relationships, the less self-esteem and confidence they will retain. Therefore, soul laws dictate that the abused will require outside sources to encourage them to stop allowing the abuse and to remove themselves from the situation.

In abuse situations, damage to the soul is not visible, but it is real and often takes longer to heal than the physical injuries. Abuse victims begin to shut down, to lose normal emotional connections and reactions. They do this to protect themselves. Denial and excuses for the abuser are often established. While in denial, the abuse only grows. No healing can begin until there is acknowledgement and removal from the situation. The longer the abused stays in an abusive situation, the greater the abuse becomes.

Soul laws dictate that it won't get better on its own. It is like a cancer that can't be stopped.

The above scenario reveals numerous soul laws. They govern the direction of forces moving in abusive circumstances. People are able to change their soul destiny when they are proactive and don't allow situations to take their "natural course." We should not buy into the belief that our future is set. The outcome of our circumstances is not predetermined. Even though we all have predispositions that affect our reactions to situations, we are not bound or locked into action or inaction because of our natural inclinations. We all retain God's mighty gift of choice. We should seek to understand soul laws in order to make wise decisions.

Spiritual Laws

Most people consider spiritual laws to be less absolute than soul laws and not even on the radar compared to physical laws. Similar to psychological soul laws, spiritual laws can't be seen, are open to interpretation, and are difficult to prove. But Scripture says spiritual laws are eternal. The physical will one day disappear; "Heaven and earth will pass away" (Matt. 24:35). That passage goes on to say "but my words will never pass away." Jesus words are eternal. They are spiritual truths that do not change. They can be trusted more than physical or soul laws.

Jesus summed up spiritual requirements for living life God's way: Love God with all you have and are, and love your neighbor as yourself. These things are what matter in eternity. The heavens and earth will pass away, but the spiritual souls of men and their deeds—will follow them to eternity. If we have accepted Jesus sacrifice, our sins will be forgiven, and we'll spend eternity with God. If we reject him, we will be eternally separated from his presence and love. God promises that heaven with him will far surpass anything we can conceive or imagine. He also explains that hell is a place away from God's presence, where there is anguish and gnashing of teeth. Living in alignment with and in submission to spiritual laws will not only make today better, it will allow us to live in his love and mercy forever.

"It is easier for heaven and earth to disappear than for the least stroke of a pen to drop out of the Law." (Luke 16:17)

World's Reality: Physical laws are unbreakable.

Spiritual Reality: Spiritual laws are greater than physical laws.

The world is full of skeptics who believe that the physical realm is all that there is. They believe that when you die, your body goes back to dust, and you are no more. They also believe that only what is seen is real, and often they live their lives accordingly—for themselves above all else, never realizing they will answer to God almighty one day. While the physical is undeniably real, it is subject to a greater reality—that of the spirit.

Jesus broke physical laws to accomplish spiritual goals. He brought healing to bodies wracked with incurable diseases; the blind, deaf, and dumb were healed. Those with seizures and demon possession were delivered. The dead were raised. He walked on water, calmed the storm, and fed five thousand with five loaves and two fish. After the Resurrection, he entered a room where the doors were locked (John 20:26). He was not in the form of a spirit; he was flesh and bone (Luke 24:39). Jesus repeatedly showed he had authority over physical laws, and that they were subject to his supreme spiritual laws.

God has embedded his spiritual laws and realities in the physical world and in our hearts. The Bible states that "The requirements of the law are written on their hearts, their consciences also bearing witness, and their thoughts now accusing, now even defending them" (Rom. 2:15). Innately, we know it is wrong to hurt other people, to lie, to be selfish, to be out of control, to manipulate or to demand our way, because God has placed his sense of justice in our hearts. We understand what is right and wrong, what is fair. Children often scream, "That's not fair." They know innately what is just. Conversely, we know it is good to help other people, to give, to care for those who can't care for themselves, to be kind and loving. It is written in our hearts.

Years of living outside of these internally placed laws will render our consciences calloused and useless. Brainwashing from others can also distort God's original spiritual laws within us. If a liar tells a lie often enough, even he begins to believe it, and he no longer feels guilt when lying. Our understanding of God's law can be distorted.

God has also kindly displayed his spiritual laws and unseen qualities in creation. Creation itself shouts God's glory, beauty, order, grandeur, majesty, and omnipotence. The earth—even in its fallen state—and heavens display spiritual qualities. What do you see when you gaze at a sunset (or sunrise) over the ocean? What qualities are found in the mighty Rockies, the incredible Grand Canyon, the thunderous Niagara Falls, the great Redwoods, or the glorious stars and galaxies? God says he is revealed in what he has made (Ps. 19:1; Rom. 1:20).

24

God Is Near

World's Reality: God doesn't care.

Spiritual Reality: God cares deeply.

Because evil and suffering exist in the world, many people believe God cannot love mankind. It is easy to understand why many who do not know God question his existence or his love. If we focus on the evil and destruction on earth, the fallen world is an ugly place. God's word explains the existence of evil and the temporary rule of Satan on Earth. But Earth's condition is our fault, not God's.

In order to be in relationship with man, God created mankind with the gift of choice. Man chose Satan's way instead of God's way and brought a curse upon humanity and all of creation. But God didn't leave us cursed for all time; he provided a way for the curse to be conquered—Christ's death on the cross. His sacrifice brings redemption to our spirits today and to all of creation one day (Rom. 8:19–22).

While God's children should focus on his centrality in their lives, the amazing paradox is found in John 3:16. Most of us know the verse: "For God so loved the world that he gave his one and only Son, that whoever believes in him shall not perish but have eternal life." The supreme one loves us so much, that he gave his life for us. It is almost unthinkable. The divine became human. He died so that we could have true life. Such a sacrifice should not be ignored.

The night Jesus was arrested he prayed, "Father, the time has come. Glorify your Son, that your Son may glorify you. For you granted him authority over all people that he might give eternal life to all those you have given him. Now this is eternal life: that they may know you, the only true God, and Jesus Christ, whom you have sent" (John 17:1–3). The purpose for Jesus death was to give us eternal life, knowing and being in relationship with the almighty. In his death and Resurrection, he glorified the Father by bridging the gulf our sin had created. He restored mankind to his intended relationship with God.

After Jesus' death and Resurrection, he sent the Holy Spirit to dwell with believers. The Holy Spirit is our comforter, advocate, guide, and spirit of truth who leads us to truth. While we should place our focus on God and realize life is about him, we can simultaneously know he is keenly focused on us, ever vigilant that we know him better and better. He lavishes us with his presence, grace, and favor when we draw near to him. And when we pull away, he continues to draw us with his kindness and Holy Spirit. He is for us.

Though God's transcendence beyond humanity is immeasurable, he is constantly mindful of each person he has created—down to the number of hairs on our head (Luke 12:7). His focus is on us. "For a man's ways are in full view of the Lord, and he examines all his paths" (Prov. 5:21) God searches and tests our hearts (Prov. 15:11, 17:3, 21:2), knows our thoughts (Prov. 15:26), and weighs our motives (Prov. 16:2). God knows us better than we know ourselves.

The love that is so mindful of our thoughts and motives is far beyond any human equivalent. Unlike the deist who thinks God started it all and is just sitting back and watching, Christians know that he is interested and involved intimately in our lives. "In his heart a man plans his course, but the Lord determines his steps" (Prov. 16:9). How can we imagine that he is far away and unconcerned with what is going on in our lives today? "Nothing in all creation is hidden from God's sight. Everything is uncovered and laid bare before the eyes of him to whom we must give account" (Heb. 4:13).

World's Reality: Letter of the law
Spiritual Reality: Spirit of the law

"Woe to you, teachers of the law and Pharisees, you hypocrites! You give a tenth of your spices—mint, dill, and cumin. But you have neglected the more important matters of the law—justice, mercy and faithfulness" (Matt. 23:23). While acts of sacrifice and generosity have their place, they are not as important to God as acts of justice, mercy, and faithfulness. "For I desire mercy, not sacrifice, and acknowledgement of God rather than burnt offerings" (Hosea 6:6). Jesus criticizes the Pharisees for following the letter of the law, but not taking care of their families (Matt. 15:5). We must clearly prioritize our spiritual life. If we place the letter of the law above all else, we risk becoming self-righteous and lacking in love. Being people of love is God's primary desire for us.

Unfortunately, our society is enslaved by the letter of the law, rather than the spirit of the law. The governmental law was set in place to secure justice and provide punishment and rehabilitation for those who do wrong. But we have become bound and shackled by the letter of the law. Too often, technicalities allow the guilty to escape conviction. Often, everyone knows the accused is guilty, but some fine letter of the law wasn't followed, so he is set free. Many times, laws that were created to bring justice, fail to do so. Our system does not cherish the standard of innocence or guilt, but bows to the letter of the law. Innocence and guilt are the logical definitive measures of justice, but we are constrained by the letter.

The Pharisees of Jesus day fell into this trap. The religious rulers hated Jesus because he broke the letter of the law—"working" (healing) on the Sabbath. The greater truth and reality was that the healing and restoration of an individual trumps the Sabbath. But the religious leaders, as is often the case today, were restrained by the letter because they did not perceive the greater truth. May God help us to move beyond religiosity into relationship and the "law of love." Holding to love and grace does not advocate sin or slothfulness in our walk with God. We must always keep in mind God's greatest commands—to love God with all we are and to love our neighbor as ourselves. With those as our primary measure and desire, God will give us the wisdom to perceive his truth and its application in our daily life.

25

My Response

World's Reality: Life is unfair, so I'll grumble and complain.

Spiritual Reality: God has given us more than we deserve.

Life is hard. Life is unfair. Life is cruel. All of these statements are true. In this life, we will be subject to evil and the corresponding results brought by sin—our own and others'. And yet we are commanded to be grateful. God is good, just, and loving. We don't deserve God's grace and mercy toward us, yet he gives it freely. His mercies are new every day. And, ultimately, good will triumph over evil and God over Satan.

Jonah grew up with an alcoholic father and co-dependent mother who was drowning in her husband's addiction. She was often so depressed she didn't get out of bed. At an early age, Jonah had to be the adult in the family, making sure his younger siblings were cared for. He made their lunches and helped them with homework. Though he loved his two sisters and little brother, he resented having adult responsibilities. Beneath his apparent maturity an angry child seethed. His dad's drunken ravings sometimes resulted in Jonah exploding in return. He'd argue with his father and end up smashing whatever was close by, or punching a hole in the wall.

When Jonah was thirteen, he and his father got into the first of many fistfights. After a fight they wouldn't talk to each other for weeks. Between brawls, Jonah became passive-aggressive and deliberately irritated his father by moving his tools, "forgetting" to do chores, and staying out past curfew.

The small satisfaction he derived from this approach didn't make him happy. Life was cruel, God was unfair, and he was miserable.

At fifteen, Jonah became a Christian at a summer day camp. Through the rest of his teen years he grew in spirit and learned to be grateful, though his situation was often grim. His dad was addicted to alcohol, and his mom had become addicted to prescription drugs. His parents weren't there for him the way parents should be, but Jonah knew God loved him and his parents, and he knew God wanted him to love his parents in spite of their deficiencies.

It took time, but God changed Jonah's resentful, angry heart into one that was grateful and able to love his parents. He realized life wasn't fair, but he had much for which to be grateful. His mom had inherited their farm that sat on rolling hills in the Ozarks. The farm was surrounded by beautiful woods and a bubbling stream. Jonah hunted and fished during season, and enjoyed God's creation all year long. The family always had enough to eat and clothes to wear. He and his sisters and brother were healthy. And above all else, he had been reconciled to his creator, and his sins were forgiven. God's grace led him to turn from his anger and embrace a grateful heart. He was thankful in spite of some negative circumstances and, on a very deep level, he was at peace and finally happy.

As is often the case, the change in Jonah began a ripple effect in changing the family dynamic. His mom became a Christian and joined a twelve-step program at church. She no longer enabled her husband, and he initially reacted badly. But after many months, he is taking a serious look at the faith of his loving wife and son. There is no guarantee he will become a believer, but the chances are much higher now that Jonah has embraced God's reality and is maintaining a grateful heart, rather than being an angry victim for the unfairness of it all.

Of all the spiritual disciplines, being thankful will have one of the greatest impacts on our attitude and perception about all that surrounds us. Hundreds of times throughout the Old and New Testament, Scripture encourages us to be thankful or give thanks or to praise God (all focusing on the positive aspects of what we have, what is good, and what is uplifting).

Being grateful is a great faith builder. When we focus on all the good things God has done and is doing in our lives and the world, we will naturally trust him to do more. Contemplating his character and action in days past builds our expectation and faith for him to continue to work in our situation today.

A grateful heart places us in proper relationship to God as one dependent on him. Being grateful or thankful implies we are showing appreciation to another outside of ourselves. It demonstrates that we are not feeling entitled or arrogant. Thankfulness acknowledges that we don't "deserve" all that God has lavished upon us, but that it is all by his great mercy and grace. Dave Ramsey, radio and TV host, always responds with a classic grateful expression when asked how he is. He replies, "Better than I deserve." And so it is.

World's Reality: It is all about us.
Spiritual Reality: It is about Him.

"It is not about you," is Rick Warren's opening statement in *The Purpose Driven Life*. This truth is counter to our understanding that we are the world's central focus. God's word states, "For from him and through him and to him are all things. To him be the glory forever!" (Rom. 11:36). He is the creator, the focus, the measure, the sustainer and the reason for our existence. It is all about him.

Americans tend to see things narcissistically. We make ourselves the measure, the beginning and the end of what the world is all about. Such thinking leads us to live in a way that barely or rarely acknowledges God's actual centrality. A deception Satan has propagated since the fall is that "You will be like God" (Gen. 3:5). While we are created in God's image, there is no mistaking that we are not to place ourselves in the position of God. The Lord's Prayer (Matt. 6:9–15) clearly proclaims that he alone is holy, provider, deliverer, omnipotent, and he alone is to be glorified.

We err seriously when we believe we can dictate to God. He is the Father, the Master, the Supreme Being. He has given us a position a little lower than the angels (Heb. 2:7), but our place remains galaxies below him, the almighty creator of the universe. We are his creatures. As beings created in His image, we have a limited ability to create and to choose good or evil. These things differentiate us from much of his creation. We don't live by instinct, like animals. We are special. We are loved.

In relationship to God, we are the children, the servants, and the worshipers; we are not the parents, the masters, or the ones worthy of worship. We should never lose our perspective on this important issue. Idols are not just made of wood and stone. Our greatest idol may be the image we see in the mirror each morning.

Many so called "prosperity" teachers and much modern "spirituality" call for us to either dictate to God or to become our own God. It is a perversion of God's truth and order in the universe. He is and always will be God supreme. While we can enjoy his gift of life and all of his creation, we cannot replace him with our superior intelligence, faith, or spirituality. We are creations; he is the creator. We are finite; he is infinite. We are unworthy; he is worthy. We are needy; he needs nothing. We are not and never will be God.

World's Reality: Look to yourself to find actualization.

Spiritual Reality: Look to God to find fulfillment.

Many in today's world claim that salvation is found within. If we just work hard enough, meditate long enough, tap into the secret law of attraction, get in touch with our inner child, channel the inner god or guide, achieve enlightenment, discover our passion, use our gifting, speak a profession of faith, correct our self-talk, or think positively our lives will be right. While some of these have elements of truth and reality, and thus benefit, none can bring salvation into our lives. The "mightiest power in the Universe"[4] they are not! They all fall far short, for salvation is not found within. It is found only through Christ Jesus, God's son. He did what none of us can do. His sacrificial death saved us from sin and separation from God. We must merely accept his free gift, for we are helpless to save ourselves. We can never be "good enough" to earn salvation. "All our righteous acts are like filthy rags" (Isa. 64:6).

As long as our focus is on saving ourselves, we will miss the mark. Yes, we need to examine our hearts and know what lies within, but we are powerless to change what we find, and if we are honest, what we find will need changing. Only God can give us a new heart. Yes, we can change our behavior and instill better habits and ways of viewing life, but only the Holy Spirit can make a selfish heart selfless, an angry heart tender, and an empty heart full. Substitutes may be found that have a temporary satisfaction, but the lasting answer is found only in God and his transforming power.

"Trust in the Lord with all your heart and lean not on your own understanding; in all your ways acknowledge him, and he will make your paths straight. Do not be wise in your own eyes; fear the Lord and shun evil" (Prov. 3:5–7). Scripture is clear: We must submit to God and seek

---

4. Rhonda Byrne, *The Secret* (New York: Atria Books, 2006), 14.

Him for our lives to "work." Anything less and we are out of line with the true order of reality.

World's Reality: My life is mine.
God's Reality: My life is His; I am a manager.

God has made each one of us a manager over our life. No one else can live life for us. No one else can choose. No one else can be held accountable for the way we live and the choices we make. Jesus loves us so much that he gave his life for us; he felt the separation from God that we should have suffered as the punishment for our sin. We should respond to this ultimate gift with our lives. God has told us to love him with all of our heart, soul, mind, and strength. But what does that mean in concrete terms?

Our stewardship includes time, money, talent, possessions, relationships, and energy. God has placed us each in charge of all of these areas of our life. We make choices every day in each of these arenas. We cannot take credit for what God has given us, only for what we do with it. One day we will be either a "good and faithful servant" or someone who refused to use what God gave us. Make your life count. Don't be afraid to use what God has entrusted to you, like the man in Jesus' parable who buried his talent (Matt. 25:25–30). Don't let fear grip your life and keep you from accomplishing the purposes for which you were created.

When we realize that we are managers and not owners of our time, talent, possessions, relationships, and energy, our attitude toward all of them will change. This is a fundamental shift in the paradigm from which most people operate. Most consider themselves the owner of all they have. They use most of the above items for their own purposes without thought of God's purposes. Rick Warren's book *The Purpose Driven Life* wonderfully outlines God's purposes for you and me. In a nutshell, we were created for God's pleasure, to worship Him, to be in relationship with his family, to become like Christ, to serve God (by serving others), and to fulfill our personal mission and the great commission. How do these objectives line-up with the goals you have set for your life?

Don't despair if you fall short. We all do. Thankfully, God is patient and gradually works in our lives so we can accomplish his purposes, rather than our own. The first step to change is recognizing that we are off track. We must understand truth before we can live truth. The reality of living for ourselves is not God's reality. He created us for his purposes and his glory. This alternate reality will bring us into the life of fulfillment that Jesus promises his followers.

Only you can choose what you do with your life. No one else can make you use your talents or possessions for God's purposes. You are in charge of your life, as a good manager is in charge of his boss's business. A bad manager spends all of his time on himself. He develops relationships only for himself. He spends his boss's money on himself, rather than the company. His daily tasks are self-promoting rather than promoting his company. He may attend a staff meeting once a week, but he is not concerned about what is being said, only that others think he is a good employee. Don't be a poor manager, but strive to be a conscientious manager of all of God's blessings in your life.

SECTION VIII: SPIRITUAL REALITY

OVERVIEW

Summary

Ultimate truth and reality belong to God alone. The more we align our lives with his truths, the more we accomplish his purposes in the world and the better our lives will be. God has wonderfully made us body, soul, and spirit. While we tend to put greatest emphasis on the physical because we can see, touch, smell, and feel it with our senses, the spiritual realities are those that will never pass away. Jesus broke many physical laws while on Earth, but kept his Father's spiritual realities, which had supreme authority.

Our understanding of our world is often misguided. We view life as being about us, rather than about God. We must keep our perspective in this crucial issue or we'll fall into blatant heresy, elevating ourselves to deity.

Many feel that God is distant and doesn't care for his creation. His word indicates just the opposite. He cares so deeply that he allowed his only son to die for us. He is intimately involved in every aspect of our lives, understanding every thought and motive, even knowing the number of hairs on our head.

The letter and spirit of the law sometime clash, and we should make sure we are focused on the more important matters of justice, mercy, and faithfulness. While many look within to find fulfillment, God is our only true source of fulfillment. A grateful heart will enable us to see all the good and undeserved things God has given us. As a steward of our time, money, talent, possessions, relationships, and energy, we must be a good manager and use them for God's purposes.

Light Reality

- The unseen is most real; spiritual laws are greater than physical laws.
- Life is all about God; God cares about us deeply.
- The spirit of the law trumps the letter of the law.
- We can find lasting fulfillment only in God.
- God has given us more than we deserve, so we should be grateful.
- My life is God's—I am just a manager.
- These nuggets of reality often play counter to our culture and natural ways of thinking. When we embrace and apply them to our lives, we align ourselves with the alternate reality—the ultimate reality—God's reality.

Dark Reality

- Those who believe that what is seen is most real—physical laws are unbreakable; life is all about them; God doesn't care; the letter of the law should rule; they should look within to find actualization; God has treated them unfairly, and that their life is their own—will suffer for living in the world's reality.
- These beliefs lead to a superficial, selfish life, far below the standard that God has available for his children.
- Life's true meaning is clouded when based on these false suppositions.
- Lasting fulfillment is absent when we live in the world's reality.

Reality Discussion Questions

1. How do you view reality?

_____

_____

2. If spiritual reality is not primary in your life, how can you shift your focus to realities that last?

_____

_____

3. Is your focus on God or yourself?

_____

_____

4. What in your life keeps you from recognizing how much God loves you?

_____

_____

5. Are you more concerned about the letter of the law than the spirit of the law?

_____

_____

If so, how can you shift your focus?

_____

_____

6. What current philosophies have you heard that indicate that you can find fulfillment from within?

_____

_____

7. How are these philosophies contrary to God's word?

_____

_____

8. For what are you grateful?

_____

_____

9. How would you grade yourself as manager of the life God has given you?

_____

_____

10. What can you do to improve your grade?

_____

_____

11. Retake the quiz at the beginning of Spiritual Reality. Did you change any of your answers? Which ones and why?

_____

_____

Prayer

Heavenly Father, thank you for giving me spiritual eyes to see the world as you see it. Help me to stay focused on the things that are real and lasting. Thank you for loving me so much that Jesus died for me. Give me wisdom to live for you, rather than for me. Help me to be a faithful manager of all that you've entrusted to me. Forgive me for the times I've trusted the world's reality. Let me begin to trust the alternate reality and to have a grateful heart. In Jesus' name, amen

Epilogue

Life's Graduation Banquet, *continued from the Prologue*

Confusion best explains the state of the ambivalent. They had lost the ability to discern what tasted good and what tasted bad. Duplicity had filled their minds. While in the light they heard the hollow laughter of friends they had left behind in the dark. As they listened to them partying, they were drawn to the revelry, but still had enough sight to realize the food in the dark did not look or smell quite as good as that in the light. And the putrid food often made them feel sick, while the food in the light strengthened them. So they raced to the light, only to be drawn again into the dark. Any measure of joy and peace was absent. Their lives were empty, not full like those feasting steadily in the light. They were never truly satisfied.

And when, on occasion, these duplicitous ones tripped and fell, it was difficult for them to rise up again because of the chains that increasingly constrained them. Eventually, many of them stayed where they had fallen in the dark and became totally blind. They joined those who believed the food in the dark was delicious and healthy, no longer feeling sick over its loathsome contents. They stopped running to the light and gained a false measure of satisfaction and peace, but only through total deception. It was the beginning of the end. They no longer took in any nourishing food and were beginning to waste away like the others around them.

On occasion, when those circling from light to dark and dark to light fell, a robed host or a person in the light helped them. And those in the light sometimes went back to the dark corners to persuade those feasting there that healthy food was available for the taking. Thus, many received help and encouragement to feast on the nourishment provided in the light and to refrain from gorging in the dark corners where only difficulty awaited them. Gradually, the chains lifted, and the layers covering their eyes melted away until they saw clearly and no longer longed for the sickening food of the dark. When this happened, there was great rejoicing.

No one was forced to eat from the tables in the light or the dark. Each participant maintained their free will to choose from the entire banquet celebration. Typically, the longer one partook of the food in the light or the dark, the less likely they would venture out to eat from the other side, but it was not impossible to stray. Those who had enjoyed a life feasting in the light would sometimes, for no apparent reason, retreat to the dark to satisfy their inappropriate appetite. And those who had languished in the dark would suddenly come to the light to dine and decide to abstain from food in the dark. It was magnificent to see that all could choose. But it was sad that not all could see what they were choosing. I began to wonder about those in the dark who couldn't see or understand what they were choosing. Had it always been that way? Were there times when they did see?

Suddenly, a trumpet sounded, shattering my thoughts. I froze in my tracks as a brilliant light—a thousand times brighter than the light in the banquet hall—shone all around. There were no longer any dark areas or shadows. All was engulfed in light. Then I heard a voice, warmer and richer than any I'd ever heard, "Your time has come." Everyone standing in the room fell to their knees. Those who were prostrate in the dark rose in submission onto their knees. All was quiet for a short time.

Then there were shouts of joy from those in the light and weeping from those who had been in the dark as they realized their true condition. The deception was gone. The light had brought sight to the blind; the truth was finally and clearly understood. The good, the nutritious, and the healthy were there for the taking, but they had chosen the bad, the putrid, and the perverted. No one had kept them from enjoying all the banquet had to offer. No one had limited their strength or growth. They had chosen, and now Life's Banquet was over. Opportunity for choosing the light path had passed. For them, time was no more. "Woe to those who call evil good and good evil, who put darkness for light and light for darkness, who put bitter for sweet and sweet for bitter" (Isa. 5:20).

Life is a gift. We each are responsible to consider how we will live the life we have been entrusted. We do not need to inflict additional pain and suffering on ourselves by choosing poorly. More than enough tragedy, sadness, and pain exists. Life's banquet offers us hope and a successful future if we choose wisely.

My goal has been to point you to the light, the reality of one who has given his life, so that we may all have true life. The entire Bible revolves around his truth. The wise will make decisions each day based on proven, eternal wisdom. Where are you living in the eight crucial realities? The darkness, the shadows, or the light?

If you would like to contact author Lissa Raines, you may e-mail her at lissa@lissaraines.com.

APPENDIX I

Resources

Al-Anon
888-4AL-ANON (25-2666)

Alcoholics Anonymous
212-870-3400
Regional numbers in phone book

American Counseling Association
800-347-6647
www.counseling.org

Celebrate Recovery
www.celebraterecovery.com
(for local meeting)

Childhelp USA
(child abuse hotline)
800-4-A-CHILD (22-4453)

Co-Dependents Anonymous
www.codependents.org (for local meeting)

Debtors Anonymous
800-421-2383
www.debtorsanonymous.org

Debt Help—Dave Ramsey
www.daveramsey.com

Divorce Care
800-489-7778
www.divorcecare.org (for local meeting)

Gam-Anon
www.gam-anon.org (for local meeting)

Gamblers Anonymous
www.gamblersanonymous.org (for local meeting)

Grief Share
800-395-5755
www.griefshare.org (for local meeting)

National Clearinghouse on Family Support and Children's Mental Health
800-628-1696

National Domestic Violence Hotline
800-799-SAFE (7233)
www.ndvh.org

National Hopeline Network
800-SUI-CIDE (784-2433)
**National Mental Health
Association**
800-969-NMHA (6642)

**National Resource Center on
Homelessness and Mental Illness**
800-444-7415

**National Resource Center on
Domestic Violence**
888-Rx-ABUSE (792-2873)
800-595-4889 (TDD)
www.endabuse.org

**National Suicide Prevention
Line**
800-273-TALK (8255)

**Rape, Abuse and Incest National
(RAIN) Network**
800-656-4673
www.rainn.org

S.A.F.E. Alternatives
800-DON'T CUT (366-8288
www.selfinjury.com

**SAMHSA's Center for Substance
Abuse Treatment**
800-662-HELP (4357)
800-487-4889 (TDD)
800-767-8432 (Spanish)

**SAMHSA's National
Clearinghouse for Alcohol and
Drug Information**
800-729-6686

Sexaholics Anonymous
866-424-8777
www.sa.org

**Sex and Love Addict
Anonymous**
www.slaafws.org (for local
meeting)

APPENDIX II

Feed on God's Word

Of crucial importance in spiritual growth is God's word. Nothing on Earth compares with the benefit we receive from feeding on it. We can feed on conversation, human relationships, books, movies, lectures, television, and thousands of other sources, but they cannot accomplish what the Bible can in our lives. The following are some things Scripture has to say about itself.

God's Word is a Measure for Thoughts and Attitudes
"For the word of God is living and active. Sharper than any double-edged sword, it penetrates even to dividing soul and spirit, joints and marrow; it judges the thoughts and attitudes of the heart" (Heb. 4:12).

The word of God is not like any other literature or book that exists. It is alive with spiritual wisdom to the depths of the soul and spirit. Most people worry about God judging our actions, but God's Word scrutinizes us way beyond actions to our thoughts, attitudes, and motives. Without God's word, we are on our own to judge whether our thoughts and attitudes are according to God's will. We are poor judges of what is acceptable to God.

God's Word has Transformation Power
"Do not conform any longer to the pattern of this world, but be transformed by the renewing of your mind. Then you will be able to test and approve what God's will is—his good, pleasing and perfect will" (Rom. 12:2).

By drinking in God's word, we are able to wash out old, fleshly, natural ways of thinking and have our minds renewed and our lives transformed. This is one of the most astounding claims of the word of God. The change starts with our minds and extends to our emotions, will, and actions. Never underestimate the power of truth working to weed out the distortions in our minds that result in the distortions in our lives.

God's Word is at Work in Us

"And we also thank God continually because, when you received the word of God, which you heard from us, you accepted it not as the word of men, but as it actually is, the word of God, which is at work in you who believe" (1 Thess. 2:13).

If we believe, God's word is at work in us. What does it mean to believe? Scripture says the demons believe and shudder (James 2:19). They mentally acknowledge that God exists, but that acknowledgement does not impact their behavior. They do not choose to submit to God or his plan for salvation. Those who believe in the sense in which 1 Thessalonians 2:13 refers go beyond a mere mental assent that God exists. They acknowledge that sin separates us from God, that Jesus paid the price for our sins with his life to reconcile us to God, that they must accept Jesus' free gift and in response turn away from sin and follow God. We do not earn our salvation, but when we are saved our lives will be different. Our deeds and changed lives are a byproduct of our salvation, not our salvation.

God's Word will Accomplish His Purposes

"My word that goes out from my mouth: It will not return to me empty, but will accomplish what I desire and achieve the purpose for which I sent it" (Isa. 55:11).

God's word is intangible, but it is the most powerful force on earth. When God spoke, the earth was created (2 Pet. 3:5). His word brings conviction and salvation, healing and life. In many circles today, Christians erroneously believe we have God's power through our spoken word. While it is important to watch our words (Matt. 12:36), we are not God. His word brings great results. But to say, "I will own a yacht and a jet and a home in Hawaii" and expect for them to materialize because of our positive profession is a perversion of truth. God does not have anything against wealth. If you have the money and buy those things, no problem (as long as you are also honoring God with your wealth and not making money your God), but to assert that your words will create those things is dangerous. You have placed yourself on God's level. We are the created, he is the creator. Do not ever confuse the two or you will be treading on Satan's territory.

God's Word is Spiritual Armor

"Take the helmet of salvation and the sword of the Spirit, which is the word of God" (Ephes. 6:17).

We are instructed to take up the word of God as part of our spiritual armor to "stand against the devil's schemes" (Ephes. 6:11) and be victorious in our spiritual life. We must know God's word to be able to apply it when faced with temptations or opposition from the enemy, Satan. Know that if you are a child of God, Satan will attack you, and the word of God will provide the answer to defeat his plan against you.

See Matthew 4:1–11 for Jesus' example in responding to the devil with Scripture. In order to do that, he had to know Scripture well. We must feed on the word regularly so that when the tempter comes, we can respond victoriously.

God's Word Is Spiritual Food

"Jesus answered, 'It is written: 'Man does not live on bread alone, but on every word that comes from the mouth of God'" (Matt. 4:4).

The word is our spiritual food. We need to eat it often. It teaches us who God is, what he has done, and what he expects of us. Without it, we can wander from the truth very quickly. Few people consider going without physical food for any length of time. Most of us are looking for physical food within hours of the last time we ate. When we don't eat, we feel weak and tired. Physical food strengthens our bodies; spiritual food, the Bible, strengthens our spirits. You cannot expect to be spiritually healthy if you are not feeding on God's word.

To digest our physical food, we merely need to put it into our body and, if all is well, our body involuntarily processes it without any other deliberate act on our part. Feeding and digesting the word of God is a little more intentional. We must read, hear (in sermons), meditate, memorize, study, and, most importantly, implement God's word in our lives. All of these actions help us to process and assimilate the word, so that we can grow strong spiritually. It is not a magical book—merely reading or quoting it will not bring about change. When combined with an open heart, God's word will connect with the soul and spirit bringing life changes no other book can create.

God's Word Purifies Us

"Sanctify them by the truth; your word is truth" (John 17:17). Jesus said, "You are already clean because of the word I have spoken to you" (John 15:3).

The truth and power of God's word cleanses us if our hearts are open to receive truth—it is the great purifier. When we receive God's word, embrace it, and apply it to our lives, it has the power to get rid of impurities and bring great change. We are no longer living by our standards of relative truth, but have embraced the never-changing logos (word). God's words bring about our transformation.

The ways of the world and the natural man are contrary to the ways of the spirit. If we just do what comes naturally or what everyone else is doing, we will fall far short. Just as our bodies need nurturing and cleansing, we must nurture our spirits by the cleansing word of God.

God's Word Brings Faith

"How, then, can they call on the one they have not believed in? And how can they believe in the one of whom they have not heard? And how can they hear without someone preaching to them? . . . Consequently, faith comes from hearing the message, and the message is heard through the word of Christ" (Rom. 10:14, 17).

Faith is heralded as necessary to know God. Without an understanding of God's plan and salvation, faith is not possible. God's word brings knowledge of God's character, purpose, and plans, so that we can have faith in him.

God's Word Outlasts Everything Else

"Heaven and earth will pass away, but my words will never pass away" (Matt. 24:35; Mark 13:31; Luke 21:33).

Three of the four gospel writers tell us that the physical world will pass away, but God's word is eternal. While we can't imagine the world without our current heaven and earth, one day it will be so. God's word remains true when all we have known no longer exists.

"The grass withers and the flowers fall, but the word of our God stands forever" (Isa. 40:8).

God's Word Sets Us Free

"To the Jews who had believed him, Jesus said, 'If you hold to my teaching, you are really my disciples. Then you will know the truth, and the truth will set you free'" (John 8:31–32).

We must know Jesus' teachings to hold to them and to live the way he wants us to. It is the starting place for our spiritual growth. As we submit to his word, he will bring greater and greater understanding and truth.

And the truth will liberate us to live forgiven lives under God's ongoing grace and mercy.

God's Word is a Lamp and a Light

"Your word is a lamp to my feet and a light for my path" (Ps. 119:105).

God's word sheds direction and clarity on our path. It illuminates the darkness and enables us to find our way. "We all stumble in many ways" (James 3:2), but God's word helps us to see his path—the one without potholes and ditches and roadblocks. Without God's illuminating word, we again are left in the dark, guessing what we should do and how we should live. God's word sheds light on our path and brings clarity to a confusing, dark world.

God's Word Is Flawless

"As for God, his way is perfect; the word of the Lord is flawless. He is a shield for all who take refuge in him" (Ps. 18:30). "Every word of God is flawless; he is a shield to those who take refuge in him" (Prov. 30:5).

It is interesting that both passages above state that God's word is flawless and both are followed with the fact that he is a shield to us when we take refuge in him. His word leads us to his protection. No one but Jesus is sinless or flawless. He and his word alone are able to be the standard for our lives. If we try to follow after a person, ultimately he or she will disappoint us in some way, so we must keep our eyes on Jesus.

Because the Bible is so old and has been translated from other languages, you might question how it can be accurate. *The God Questions* by Hal Seed and Dan Grider deals with the uniqueness, accuracy, and truth of Scripture. Given all the evidence, there is only one conclusion—the Bible is indeed the inspired word of God.

God's Command about God's Word

"Let the word of Christ dwell in you richly as you teach and admonish one another with all wisdom, and as you sing psalms, hymns and spiritual songs with gratitude in your hearts to God" (Col. 3:16).

In order to let the word dwell richly in us, we must read and study the Bible, which enables us to live a life in God's light realities.

Conclusion about God's Word

The Word of God is central to our spiritual growth. It should not be discounted or downplayed. It is the living word of God, bringing depth and power to our spiritual life. Allow the Word of God to empower you for a life of success in his kingdom.

APPENDIX III

Things God Hates or Detests

A perverse man (Prov. 3:32)

Haughty eyes (Prov. 6:17)

Lying tongue / lying lips (Prov. 6:17; 12:22)

Hands that shed innocent blood (Prov. 6:17)

A heart that devises wicked schemes (Prov. 6:18)

Feet that are quick to rush into evil (Prov. 6:18)

A false witness who pours out lies (Prov. 6:19)

A person who stirs up dissension (Prov. 6:19)

Pride (Prov. 8:13)

Arrogance (Prov. 8:13)

Evil behavior (Prov. 8:13)

Perverse speech (Prov. 8:13)

Men of perverse heart (Prov. 11:20)

The sacrifice of the wicked (Prov. 15:8)

The way of the wicked (Prov. 15:9)

The thoughts of the wicked (Prov. 15:26)

The proud of heart (Prov. 16:5)

Acquitting the guilty and condemning the innocent (Prov. 17:15)

Dishonesty (Prov. 20:23)

Robbery and iniquity (Isa. 61:8)

The wicked and those who love violence (Ps. 11:5)

APPENDIX IV

Quiz Answers

Multiple Choice Stories

The multiple choice stories are a tool to encourage reflection on some of the issues discussed in that section. Below are the letters corresponding to the **best** answers. Following the best answer is a brief explanation. You may choose a different answer or a response that is not listed. Sometimes several different options could bring about a positive result. Know why you believe the solution you have chosen is the best and be able to defend it! Our choices in life should be deliberate, rather than passive. God has given us logic, wisdom, and common sense. Let us not waste any of these and incur self-imposed "soul toll."

Section I: Relationship Realities

1. a
How a prospective spouse treats others is crucial to evaluating their character. Character can change, but rarely changes quickly. Even though Anthony treats Samantha well or if he temporarily changes for her (b, c, and d), you cannot assume that indicates improved character. Most people can fake it for a while. She has seen his true colors.

2. d
Sparks can be rekindled. It may take the help of a professional if the relationship has significant issues. Divorce is reserved for extreme issues. A general dissatisfaction with marriage is not one of them.

3. a

Abuse or uncontrollable anger, for whatever reason, must be addressed. Doing nothing (b) is an enabling position. Fighting back (c) will escalate the situation with possible negative legal ramifications. An intervention (d) will not help without addressing core issues.

Section II: God's Will

1. b

Your answer here will primarily be based on your personality and what is most important to you. If an option is morally wrong or you feel that God is saying "no," don't do it. If you believe God is leading you a particular way, do it (in big decisions, also seeking Godly counsel is appropriate). If you have prayed for leading, but have not received specific guidance, I believe God allows you the liberty to choose between available opportunities.

2. c

Even if God did speak to the person you are dating, you need to know for yourself that the relationship has long term potential. Time is crucial in knowing a person well. Until we see a prospective spouse with friends, family and in a variety of situations, we may not understand what we are getting ourselves into. Marriage is one of the most significant commitments you will make in your life. Don't rush into it.

3. b

While God does discipline his children (a), we cannot automatically assume that someone is out of God's will when misfortune comes their way. Bad things happen to everyone. Of course "karma" (c) is not a Christian concept. In a general sense we reap what we sow, especially spiritually and eternally, but not necessarily in this life. God is not causing all of Amanda's problems (d). Following God will eliminate a lot of self-imposed difficulty, but does not guarantee easy sailing. We live in a fallen world. Good and bad befall us all. Gratefulness for what we do have can bring a positive perspective.

Section III: Personality Realities

1. f
Limiting John's teaching methods (a) would indicate he is wrong to be different. Personality preferences, reflected here in teaching methods, are neither right nor wrong, but merely different. Other teachers may be jealous (b), but inaction rarely resolves issues. Unaddressed, they tend to get worse.

2. c
While answers "a," "b," and "d" may bring some positive results, direct communication about the issue among the parties involved is usually the most successful option.

3. c
If you chastise Tiffany or Justin for their personality preferences (a and b), you indicate one is right and one is wrong, rather than different. Understanding each other's needs and preferences and learning how to compromise will help long term. While it is true that basic personality doesn't change (d), it is possible for two very different people to have a successful relationship.

Section IV: Real Authority

1. b
Although paralegals are on a higher pay scale than Ashley (a), she does not answer to them. She should notify her supervising attorney about the problem, so he can address the issue with Daniel (c). Quitting (d) is not the answer. Every job has pressures and difficulties.

2. c
We are not God (a); we cannot create reality. While our thoughts and attitudes can influence our lives, we cannot create deep lasting fulfillment through visualization. Nor can we meditate our way to lasting peace – (b). Visualizing and meditating don't deal with the sin that separates us from God. True enduring peace is found only in a redeemed relationship with our creator. While vacations (d) are beneficial, they only provide a temporary pleasure, not lasting fulfillment.

Section V: Money Realities

1. d

Avoiding collections (c) is tempting, but will only make matters worse. Deal with debt head-on. Cut expenses, increase income (if possible) and make a plan to reduce debt, even if it is only a little each pay period. Do something!

2. b

This is a version of a widespread scam that actually happened to me (after my third refusal to pay the nanny, I never heard from him again!). Do not cash a check and send or give it to another person/ company/ lottery, etc., via cash, cashier's check, or money order (a). The checks are fake, although they often look real and may initially be accepted by your bank. They will bounce, and you will be out the money you sent back or gave to another person.

3. b

You could refuse Courtney (a) or insist she pay you (d) before loaning her more money, but that wouldn't be a long term fix. Helping her to set up and stick to a budget will eliminate her problem and your problem! If she doesn't allow your help, then (a or d) is your best option. Continuing to loan (c) or give her money is the worst thing you can do for Courtney. You will be enabling her to continue to be irresponsible.

Section VI: Lifestyle Realities

1. d

Rather than avoiding any of his friends (a, b, and c), Bill should confront the situation head on. Each of his friends can then choose to continue the friendship or not. That is their prerogative. Speaking the truth in love is always the best choice.

2. d

If you find yourself in a compromising situation, the best option is to physically remove yourself. An even better option is to guard you heart and not allow yourself to progress to that point! But if you are tempted, leave the premises. You don't have to go to the extreme of leaving the city (a). And under no circumstances should you allow yourself to be involved an affair (b). So there is no need to ask for advice from your friends (d) since an affair is not an option.

Section VII: The Dark Reality of Lies

1. c

Lies have a ripple effect and multiple lies have multiple ripples. They hurt the liar and those lied to in numerous ways. See chapter 21.

2. b

Nicole is compromising her integrity to promote herself. Instead of lying, she could have revised her resume to reflect her personal strengths and accomplishments at the jobs she previously held, rather than fabricate experience. If she gains employment under false pretenses, she will lose trust and possibly even her job. Her lies are much more serious than "white lies" (a). She isn't trying to protect herself (c) or maliciously hurt another person (d).

Section VIII: Spiritual Reality

1. e

Bitterness is never a right (a) and hurts the bitter party more than anyone else. If Jake restores his relationship with his mother (c), it is a good thing, but does not change his standing with God. He must acknowledge that God is his source (b) and accept Jesus' redeeming work. This alone gives us a righteous standing with God.

2. c

Salvation lies in our acceptance of God's provision through Jesus. All other paths (a, b, and d) are an attempt at saving ourselves and are worthless.

3. c

When we acknowledge that all we have is God's, we can't justify keeping it all to ourselves. We will each answer to God one day for what we have done with what he has provided.

True and False Answers

All but one statement in each of the true/false quizzes are "false." Most of the questions embody widely accepted, but false cultural or false "American Christian" beliefs, so you may have initially answered many of the questions as "true." You will find the answers for each question within the chapters of that section. Of course, some true/false answers may be open for interpretation based on how you understood the statement. Without the opportunity for personal dialogue, we will have to agree to disagree. The quizzes help you to evaluate what you believe and the chapters help you to clarify those beliefs. And your beliefs will drastically influence many of your choices every day. When you have an accurate understanding of the eight realities, you will have the best opportunity for success in this life and the one to come. May God bless your life as you daily choose to follow him.

The following are the **true** statement in each quiz:

Section I: Relationship Realities   #10

Section II: God's Will   #8

Section III: Personality Realities   #4

Section IV: Real Authority   #5

Section V: Money Realities   #4

Section VI: Lifestyle Realities   #9

Section VII: The Dark Reality of Lies   #7

Section VIII: Spiritual Reality   #2